INTO *light*
THE

THE ACADEMIC & SPIRITUAL LEGACY OF
DR. HOWARD MALMSTADT

JOHN FEAVER

INTO *Light*
THE

THE ACADEMIC & SPIRITUAL LEGACY OF
DR. HOWARD MALMSTADT

YWAM
PUBLISHING
P.O. Box 55787 / Seattle, WA 98155

YWAM Publishing is the publishing ministry of Youth With A Mission. Youth With A Mission (YWAM) is an international missionary organization of Christians from many denominations dedicated to presenting Jesus Christ to this generation. To this end, YWAM has focused its efforts in three main areas: (1) training and equipping believers for their part in fulfilling the Great Commission (Matthew 28:19), (2) personal evangelism, and (3) mercy ministry (medical and relief work).

For a free catalog of books and materials, contact

YWAM Publishing
P.O. Box 55787, Seattle, WA 98155
(425) 771-1153 or (800) 922-2143
www.ywampublishing.com

Into the Light: The Academic and Spiritual Legacy of Dr. Howard Malmstadt
Copyright © 2007 by John A. Feaver

12   11   10   09   08   07   10   9   8   7   6   5   4   3   2   1

Published by YWAM Publishing, a ministry of Youth With A Mission
P.O. Box 55787
Seattle, WA 98155

ISBN-13: 978-1-57658-411-8
ISBN-10: 1-57658-411-9

Library of Congress Cataloging-in-Publication Data
Feaver, John A.
  Into the light : the academic and spiritual legacy of Dr. Howard Malmstadt /
by John A. Feaver.
      p. cm.
  Includes bibliographical references and index.
  ISBN-13: 978-1-57658-411-8 (pbk. : alk. paper)
  ISBN-10: 1-57658-411-9 (pbk. : alk. paper)
  1. Malmstadt, Howard V., 1922–2003. 2. Christian biography. 3. Youth with a Mis-
sion, Inc. 4. Scientists—Religious life. I. Title.
  BR1725.M25F43 2007
  277.3'082092—dc22
  [B]   2007007960

Printed in the United States of America

To my parents, Douglas and Margaret Feaver, who were the first to show me how to serve God with excellence, humor, and love.

Contents

Acknowledgments 9

Introduction 11

1. Strong Foundations 13

2. Finding God in Times of War and Peace 19

3. The Chemistry of Teamwork 29

4. A Passion for Teaching 41

5. The Pursuit of Excellence 51

6. A Courageous Transition 57

7. Laying New Foundations 69

8. A Passion for People 83

9. Innovations for Missions 91

10. Water for Life 103

11. Homecoming 111

12. The Malmstadt Legacy 121

Afterword 129

Key Articles and Books 131

Notes 135

Photographs 138

Acknowledgments

The writing of this book started out as a "calling" of sorts but quickly became a labor of love. As I reflect over all those who helped in researching and reworking the manuscript, it is abundantly clear that I could not have done this on my own.

My first thanks go to the Malmstadt family, who graciously accepted the offer of a novice writer to write the story of Howard's life. As they did for so many years in his life, they have generously shared him yet again through me with you, the reader.

Scott and Sandi Tompkins were my first cheerleaders, and they have put in countless hours over the course of this project in helping with research and writing advice. Scott in particular took my efforts and transformed them into what you are about to read. Like many others, I have learned so much from this wonderful couple.

Howard's students have embraced this project enthusiastically, beginning with our meeting at Pittcon 2004. In particular, I want to thank Gary Hieftje (pronounced Heef-ya) for his help in making contacts with others in that special "family" and Stan Crouch for patiently helping this scientific layman to understand Howard's work and to explain it in simple terms.

As an analytical chemist and fellow YWAMer, Derek Chignell has helped tirelessly, giving his unique perspective as one of the few who bridged both major segments of Howard's life. His comments on numerous drafts have been unfailingly timely and insightful.

Tom Bragg of YWAM Publishing encouraged my vision in the early days, and Warren Walsh and Luann Anderson have helped see this down the home stretch to the finish line. I especially appreciate their enthusiasm for the value of telling Howard's story to new generations.

I spoke and exchanged emails with many who knew Howard much better than I did at the outset. You are too numerous to list here, but thanks to each of you for sharing your glimpses into the life of this exceptional man.

I also want to thank those who committed to pray with me throughout this project. I know you would prefer to remain nameless, but nonetheless you share in the blessing of seeing Howard's life inspire many others to pursue God with diligence in their own lives.

Finally, I thank my wife, Gail, for standing with me from the first time I mentioned the crazy idea, repeatedly covering home base when I was in writing mode, and even supporting my solo "book trip" to Hawaii. I treasure you as my life partner and best friend.

Introduction

As I walked through the cavernous halls of the Chicago Convention Center on March 8, 2004, passing hundreds of eager scientists and displays of the latest in esoteric research equipment, I felt hopelessly out of place. The annual Pittcon Conference on Analytical Chemistry attracts many of the world's most brilliant scientists, and my technical credentials as a systems engineer in communications at AT&T seemed way too flimsy for admittance to this august company.

Yet once I entered the symposium meeting room, I sensed the same warmth and acceptance I had known in the man these scientists had come to honor—Dr. Howard V. Malmstadt. I first met Howard years earlier while serving with Youth With A Mission (YWAM) in Hawaii, and although I did not have the privilege of working directly with him, his example had profoundly influenced my life. Pittcon had set a full-day symposium on the academic legacy of this man, who had passed away the previous July. I sat in awe as first-, second-, and even third-generation students stood up to honor a man they described as one of the twentieth century's greatest scientists and educators, in many ways the "father" of modern analytical chemistry. These students, now renowned scientists in their own right, choked back tears as they described Howard Malmstadt as the "brother they never had."

Months earlier, a YWAM conference in Singapore called Synergy 2003 also had set aside time to honor the memory of Dr.

Malmstadt. On that occasion, the gathering included missionaries serving in far-flung parts of the world, with a wide range of cultural backgrounds. The speakers alluded to Howard's impressive scientific accomplishments, although their focus was on his foundational work on the University of the Nations, a global university committed to training missionaries to reach cultures through the full spectrum of academic studies. Again, a number of the speakers struggled with tears as they spoke with great fondness of Howard Malmstadt.

What was it about this man that united these two disparate groups in a common bond of respect and affection for him? Dr. H. V. "High Voltage" Malmstadt had for decades unlocked the mysteries of electrons, magnetism, and other power sources. Yet for all his great discoveries, all his intellectual prowess, and all his academic and humanitarian achievement, what stood out most to those who knew him was his amazing humility and love for people. You could not know Howard Malmstadt without being energized by his enthusiasm, his kindness, and his creativity. He made all feel equally valued as human beings—from the lowliest freshman student to the most eminent scientist or educator.

Dr. Malmstadt made many scientific discoveries, but his greatest discovery and the source of his love for people came early in his life when he had recognized that there was no greater force in the universe than the love of God. As a boy, he opened his heart to that love, and he reflected it to countless others throughout his long and productive life. It is an honor and a privilege to share his story so that future generations may know this great man.

In writing this book, I conducted numerous interviews (by e-mail and in person) with family, friends, and colleagues of Dr. Howard Malmstadt. Unless otherwise noted, all quotations in this book are from those interviews.

I.

Strong Foundations

Learning is not attained by chance, it must be sought for with ardor and attended to with diligence.

— ABIGAIL ADAMS

*F*our-year-old Howard held his breath as he shut the door. He heard nothing from the back of the house where his mother was; his father had already headed off to the family store. *So far, so good.* He pulled his jacket tightly around him and decided to button it up. The fall breeze already had a touch of winter in it.

Howard headed in the direction he had watched his big brother, Robert, take before, and soon the schoolhouse was in sight. Careful to stay out of sight, he went from room to room, peeking in until he found what he was looking for—Robert's class in session. Howard watched it all triumphantly.

He had wanted desperately to go to school, and now he had found a way to at least watch it. After a few days of this, the teachers decided to set aside the rules and let him join the class, which spanned kindergarten through second grade.

Thus, in 1926, began the educational adventure of Howard Malmstadt in the northern Midwest town of Marinette, Wisconsin. This Malmstadt family story illustrates Howard's love of learning—a passion that lasted the rest of his life.

Howard V. "High Voltage" Malmstadt was one of those people who start life in high gear. No doubt his birthplace energized
his youthful sense of wonder and provided the first channels for his
relentless resourcefulness. In 1922, when Howard arrived as the
second child of immigrants Guy and Nellie Malmstadt, Marinette
was still a thriving port community on Lake Michigan's Green
Bay. Most of the town's income came from the Great Lakes com-
merce of lumber, iron ore, and grain. This bounty flowed up and
down the Menominee River, which formed not only the dividing
line between Marinette and the rival town of Menominee but also
the border between Wisconsin and Michigan. Through these por-
tals poured a continuous stream of loggers, traders, miners, and
barge runners—many of them Scandinavians like the Malmstadts.

In fact, there were so many Scandinavians in the area that the
family changed its name from Swanson to Malmstadt when they
emigrated from Malmo, Sweden. Thus "Malm" and "stadt" (city)—
from the city of Malmo. Nellie's grandparents and parents were
German. Guy's mother was French. So Howard's heritage was
essentially half German, one-fourth Swedish, and one-fourth
French. A good American mix.

Howard's father, Guy, owned and managed a neighborhood
grocery store in Marinette. As the town grew, so did his business,
which he expanded several times during his ownership. Even when
some of the nearby iron mines played out and the lumber trade
slowed, he still managed to keep his business on solid ground.
Like other Midwesterners from immigrant stock, the Malmstadts
raised Howard and Robert with a strong Protestant work ethic, a
rock-solid faith in God, devotion to family, and a belief in America as a land of boundless opportunity. Nellie Malmstadt, herself
a teacher before getting married, saw education as a key to tapping
into that opportunity and taught her sons the joys of reading,
through storybooks, classic novels, and the Bible.

The two Malmstadt boys were remarkably different, and Guy
and Nellie were proud of both of them. Bob was a handsome little blue-eyed blond. Stoic in personality and conservative in

nature, he was careful with his money, careful with just about everything he did. By contrast, Howard was the consummate risk taker, full of energy, good in sports, and confident that whatever opportunity came up, he could turn it to his advantage. Early on, Howard gave his parents many anxious moments, climbing a telephone pole on one occasion and walking the railing of the church balcony on another. The brothers' obvious differences kept them from being close friends, but Nellie Malmstadt did her best to see that both felt affirmed and loved.

Howard worked in his father's store along with Robert and his mother, thus picking up a sense for business that later helped to set him apart from the majority of scientists. One day in the store, Howard was sent to the basement to weigh and bag up potatoes. Time passed, and when he did not reappear, someone was sent to check on him. He was discovered rigging up a machine of sorts to do the weighing/bagging chore—one of his first of many attempts to create an instrument to simplify the task at hand.

Howard flourished in high school academics and sports. He excelled in football as a quarterback and had dreams of becoming a football coach. He was a very popular jock and at the top of his class, especially in math and science but also in extracurricular activities such as debating team. One uncharacteristic blip in his record of achievement was missing Eagle Scout rank due to not completing a bird-watching assignment. This could be explained either by his extremely busy sports and academic schedules or by his lifelong reluctance to be honored in any public way.

When it came time to choose a college, Howard sought the counsel of his parents and extended family, particularly an uncle who was a beloved math teacher in nearby Menominee. The family had been a crucial support system for his many endeavors in high school, so it was not surprising that Howard wanted to study closer to home. Therefore, he chose the University of Wisconsin, also because his brother, Robert, was already there. Howard hoped that his dreams of becoming a football coach were about to be fulfilled. However, before classes started, he fell and broke his arm in

a pickup football game. When it came time to register, he switched
his major to chemistry. As his wife would comment many years
later, "It was a big fork in the road."

Indeed, for the rest of his life Howard would spend little time
on playing fields and much more in classrooms and labs.

Howard Malmstadt was never one to waste time bemoaning
or resisting change. If a man's life can be compared to a river, then
an important measure of its power is what happens when con-
fronted by a boulder. For some, the flow of the river is diverted to
eddies, becoming stagnant pools. For others, the surge of the river
continues past the boulder, taking new directions and creating
new channels for its energy. Howard was among the latter. Doing
far more than accepting change, he embraced it, focusing his legendary energy into whatever productive channels opened before
him and drawing others along as well.

Howard was a third-year chemistry student at the University
of Wisconsin when the United States was pulled abruptly into
World War II by the bombing of Pearl Harbor. As for thousands
of others in his generation, this unexpected "boulder" threatened
to derail his academic and career plans. His top grades at Wisconsin almost guaranteed him a good-paying job in industry upon
his graduation, and now his dreams of a job, a home, and family
were unraveled by events outside his control. Howard pressed on
with his studies, determined to graduate if possible.

In modern conflicts like Vietnam and Iraq, college campuses
have been havens for dissent and resistance to war, but not so in
1943 when Howard was working to finish his chemistry degree.
With battles raging across Europe, Asia, and the Pacific, the threat
to freedom spurred Americans to unprecedented support of the
war effort. Everyone was needed in one capacity or another. In the
case of the Malmstadt brothers, their sense of duty was joined with
the sense of calling that they learned from their Presbyterian
upbringing. God-given talents are meant to be used as God
directs. Bob enlisted in the army in 1942 and was shipped off to
Europe. When Howard was in his senior year, it became apparent
that he would soon be following his brother into the service.

Part of the U.S. military's recruitment strategy at the time was for Selective Service officials to visit colleges and administer aptitude tests to every male in sight. Howard tested well for electronics and was recruited by the U.S. Navy for training in a new technology called radar. So, after receiving his BS degree in 1943, he was commissioned as an ensign and sent to the Massachusetts Institute of Technology (MIT) Radiation Laboratory (RadLab) and later to Princeton University's Naval Radar School.

RadLab was formed fourteen months prior to the United States' entry into World War II to explore the promising technology of microwave electronics, especially for communication purposes. In World War II, the RadLab deployed almost half of the radar used in the war, encompassing over one hundred different radar systems and a staggering $1.5 billion worth of equipment. Howard was among the first groups of officers trained in this promising technology.

The young ensign thrived in the MIT classes. In addition to the fascinating technology of radar and its timely applications, what especially captured Howard's attention was the success of two RadLab teaching methods—"modular" courses and "immersion" training. By planning a course in modules, which could be rearranged with other modules to serve different purposes, the students could benefit from a course better customized to their own backgrounds and interests. In immersion training, an intensive mix of lectures, demonstrations, and hands-on lab experiments led quickly to a strong grasp of the subject material. Howard saw how effective these methods were for enabling a person to fully grasp and productively use the newfound knowledge and later called it "the most effective teaching I've ever had." As a bonus, the class developed a spirit of unity around a strong sense of common purpose. "We found that as we worked closely in unified teams, there were continuous breakthroughs," Howard said.[1]

Years later, Howard would apply these insights to classes and teams made up of men and women from around the world.

Upon completion of his radar training, Howard was awarded the rank of second lieutenant and assigned to the Pacific theater of the war, serving as radar officer for the USS *Wilkes* (DD441 division of destroyers). Howard's war experiences would shake him to the core, stretching him far beyond what he would have thought possible. In many ways, he was thrown into the deep end, to the front lines of the last great naval battles of World War II.

2.

Finding God in Times
of War and Peace

*As Americans, we go forward, in the service of our country, by the
will of God.*

— FRANKLIN D. ROOSEVELT

*Japanese kamikaze planes were coming out of the sky by the dozens;
planes turned into terrifying bombs guided by suicidal pilots. Nearby
ships had already been seriously damaged the day before. Howard and
the other men on the ship were tense, unsure if they would survive this battle. Howard tried to get some rest on his bunk. There in his stateroom,
God spoke words of comfort and wisdom to him.*

*Howard survived what became known as the battle of Okinawa, but
he never forgot what he witnessed that day.*

When Lieutenant Malmstadt arrived in Pearl Harbor in June
1944, the great Honolulu naval base was abuzz with whispers
about a vast amphibious assault on an island chain just south of
Japan. He did not yet know it, but he would soon be headed to
these mysterious islands to become a player in the bloody drama
that would extend across the soon-to-be-famous islands of Saipan,
Iwo Jima, Guam, and Okinawa.

Underway at sea was a 635-ship armada steaming through
the western Pacific. Plans and maps marked SECRET: Operation

Forager were being studied and restudied by men of rank: navy, marine, and army flag officers, veterans of two and a half years of combat with Japanese imperial forces. The Americans sensed victory and an end to the colossal slaughter called World War II. According to the commander in chief of the U.S. fleet, Admiral Ernest J. King, the Mariana Islands were the key to the central Pacific. His finger pressed a map and traced the invisible lines of communication for Japan's "Inner South Seas Empire." Air Force General Henry H. "Hap" Arnold saw the Marianas as an ideal forward base for the new B-29 Superfortresses that could each carry ten thousand pounds of ordnance twelve hundred miles—all the way to Tokyo—and release them with a vengeance.[1]

The Japanese also knew well the strategic value of the Marianas. Admiral Toyoda declared to his men, "The fate of the empire rests on this one battle. Every man is expected to do his utmost."[2]

Lieutenant Malmstadt was confounded by the secrecy he encountered at Pearl Harbor. He was given a sheet telling him to report to a particular place near Pearl Harbor, after which he would leave at midnight on a flight to an unspecified destination. When he got there, he went to a navy office and asked the whereabouts of Destroyer Division 14. At first they had no idea, but the next day someone suggested it might be in Tarawa, about fifteen hundred miles from there. Howard remembered: "I started chasing that ship—at least the rumors of where the ship might be— all over the Pacific. Finally I thought, *This is crazy.* I remembered that on that seaplane I had slept on mailbags. I asked, 'Where are those mailbags going?' I was told they were going to go in the next few days to Saipan."

Howard hitched a ride on that flight as it flew east toward a battle that was already under way. "I moved very cautiously when I got off near Saipan because the war was going on. I asked about Destroyer Division 14. They said that in two days, at midnight, there would be some ships coming in about thirty miles offshore. 'That's where we're going to start delivering those mailbags,' I was told." It occurred to Howard that his division might be in that battle group, so he asked to be taken out to those ships, visible in the moonlight. They first encountered the USS *Enterprise,* a three-block-long aircraft carrier. Howard continued, "I just called up to the guys on the rail above, 'Is Destroyer Division 14 attached with you in any way?' They said, 'Oh yeah, it's right over there.' I began realizing that with all those destroyers and all those ships being in one location, it had to be top secret. That's why no one knew where they were."

In their desperate effort to stop this U.S. fleet, the Japanese launched a new weapon—kamikaze pilots, who out of loyalty to the emperor were willing to fly into enemy ships on suicide missions. The Allied strategy of the day involved placing the destroyers with radar in a line facing the enemy, miles ahead of the rest of the ships. These were called "radar picket" ships. Because the ship at the front of the screen was the most vulnerable, they would take turns at that position. The USS *Wilkes* and other radar picket ships served as an early-warning system, alerting the ships farther back to the arrival of the kamikaze planes. In this way, the planes could be shot down before they could crash into the troop ships. Howard quickly saw how radar, radio, and teamwork, motivated by the life-and-death crisis, worked together to win the battle.

For Lieutenant Malmstadt the most terrifying time of the campaign was the battle of Okinawa in April 1945. Their division was being attacked by kamikazes numbering in the hundreds. Even if they managed to knock down ten or twenty at a time, more would keep coming. Howard recalled:

> Everyone on the ship was under tremendous tension.... I remember one night coming back from my battle station to catch some sleep. Suddenly I heard a voice up above my bunk. It was the words of the Twenty-Third Psalm: "Even though I walk through the valley of the shadow of death, I will fear no evil, for you are with me; your rod and your staff, they comfort me."
>
> I kept hearing these words over and over. I thought maybe I had passed out. But I was awake, and I felt God was reminding me of what I had learned in Sunday school.

But it wasn't Sunday school any longer. The ships next to us the night before had been attacked by over fifty kamikazes. Both had been hit badly. That had raised the tension even higher on our ship. I was going to pray [for our safety], and then it was as if a voice said, *Don't pray for your own ship.* I didn't ever hear in Sunday school that you could ask God what to pray about. However, I knew it that day. So I asked God, "What do I pray about?" It was very clear that I should pray for the tension on our ship to be removed. Within a few minutes we were called back to battle stations. I'd never known a prayer to be answered more quickly. [The men] arrived at their stations smiling and talking even though they knew [this battle] might be their last. I knew God wanted my attention. It was a strange way of getting it, but when I got back to my room, I immediately picked up my Bible and blew the dust off it. I opened it, and the words of John 14:6 seemed to jump off the page: "Jesus answered, 'I am the way and the truth and the life. No one comes to the Father except through me.'"

That was significant to me, because during my university days in talking with people of different religions, they always said, "How can Jesus be *the only way?*" I didn't have to question that anymore. It wasn't words jumping off the page. It wasn't Jesus talking to Thomas to answer his question. It was the living Lord speaking to me. I had a gift of faith at that time. I learned other things in those four years, but nothing compared with that divine revelation. I felt the presence of God so closely.

Some soldiers experience what are called "foxhole conversions," in which they encounter God in the midst of stressful wartime situations but revert to their old ways after the danger passes. Not so with Howard Malmstadt. These Okinawa experiences cemented a commitment to God that began in his youth. And this new and personal way of relating with God formed the foundation on which the rest of his life was built, including establishing a university that spanned many countries across the world.

The Okinawa victory cost the U.S. Navy dearly. Over 4,000 sailors were killed, and another 875 were wounded. Marine casualties totaled 3,244 dead and over 2,000 wounded.[3] USS *Wilkes,* which earned ten battle stars in action across the Atlantic, North Africa, New Guinea, Philippines, Marianas and Okinawa campaigns, survived once again.[4] But nearby Howard Malmstadt's ship the wreckage was staggering. Burning ships spewed smoke and oil; floating bodies and debris littered the sea. "We learned that 162 of our ships were hit in Okinawa," Howard recalled. Horrific as the battles of Saipan, Leyte Gulf, Iwo Jima, and Okinawa had been, an even more frightful challenge faced the fleet in the weeks that followed. When the USS *Wilkes* was released from Okinawa, it joined a task force moving north to prepare for the invasion of Japan. "We knew they still had thousands of planes they could send as kamikazes. It was estimated that we would lose about one million men in a full-scale invasion. The Japanese would lose four to five million. With the information we had, we recognized that landing on Japan would cause a major slaughter."

News came one fateful day that a huge bomb had been dropped on the Japanese city of Hiroshima; then ten days later another bomb was dropped on Nagasaki. Howard predicted that the war would be over within two weeks of the bombing of Hiroshima. Others dissented, saying it was just a big bomb. Howard pushed his point: "I said it was an *atomic* bomb. I didn't know much about atomic energy, but what I'd heard in my last physical chemistry lab before going into the navy was scary. Truman had to make the decision to drop those bombs. And as horrible as they were, they probably reduced the death toll from five or six million people down to about five hundred thousand."

Howard rarely spoke of the horrors he saw in those last months of the war. He was apparently not emotionally or physically scarred by the war, as were so many other veterans. "He was always redemptive in the lessons he took from life, seeing God's sovereignty at work in his own life and in many others," his university colleague Markus Steffen comments. One of the few times he showed emotion over his experiences was when his friend Sharon Carrington described an April 2003 tour of Saipan: "The tour guide took our group to Banzai Cliff and Suicide Cliff, where many Japanese soldiers had committed *seppuku* (suicide) by jumping off the cliffs to their deaths to avoid losing face by being captured. As I told Howard of my experience, tears welled in his eyes. 'It was so hard!' he said."

Clearly, Howard carried the pain of the war years, much as do veterans of that and other wars before and since. Despite this, the war memories Howard related to others usually came out in positive and constructive ways. He often told his students about an admiral who had addressed his radar class before they joined the war. The admiral said, "How well you listen—how well you learn—could be a matter of life and death for thousands of people."[5] Lieutenant Malmstadt never forgot that. As the war progressed, and for the rest of his life, he learned everything he could to do the best job possible.

One such incident happened early on in his Pacific fleet service: "I was attached to the commodore of the task force. He called me in one day and said, 'You're maintenance officer for the task force.' I hadn't learned all about the navy protocol, so I said, 'I don't know what a maintenance officer does.' He shot back at me, using some words I wouldn't repeat. Then he said, 'You've got less than 24 hours to find out.'" Howard decided he should make an effort to reach out to those maintaining the ships. "I first tried to identify with all of the hard work they have to do to maintain these ships. Then in the process I started learning what maintenance is all about," Howard related. Howard continued to care for any maintenance people he encountered for the rest of his life. He saw all the different systems and technologies working together to make the critical difference in life-and-death situations. Later on, this would prove to be very useful in thinking through the design of a university from the ground up.

As a guest teacher in a class many years later, he said, "Never underestimate the impact of one person in the place God has called him to be." The students commented on that quote for weeks afterward.

Howard had not only survived his experiences in the navy but grown in many ways through them: As a Christian, as a leader, and as a scientist. He carried the lessons learned on the battlefield with him for the rest of his life and shared them generously with many others over the years.

As he left the Pacific, he had no idea that he would return many years later on a very different assignment.

When Howard returned Stateside after the end of the war in 1945, he was asked to join the staff of the Naval Radar School at Treasure Island in California as a supervisor in the Department of Electronic Fundamentals, holding the rank of second lieutenant.

His time at Treasure Island awakened another interest in Howard's life. In the college-age singles group at the Presbyterian Church of Berkeley, he met a young woman named Carolyn Gay Hart, then known as Gay to distinguish her from her roommate, also named Carolyn. She describes her first impression of young Lieutenant Malmstadt:

> I was a senior at Berkeley and on the greeting committee, sitting at the sign-in desk. In the midst of a room full of young people, many in military uniforms, [Howard] seemed to stand out for me with his Scandinavian accent, his courtesy...not to mention that he was very handsome in his navy officer uniform. The next several months we made arrangements to see each other [in group settings] and had dates with just the two of us.

Howard commented later that at their first meeting, Carolyn was able to pronounce his name properly, which seemed like a "good sign." Furthermore, she had spelled his hometown correctly at that first encounter. Another good sign. In the coming weeks he had plenty more good signs that this brown-haired California girl with the bright mind, ready laugh, and uncommon spiritual depth was a match for him.

The two were parted in the summer of 1946, when Howard returned to Wisconsin to see his family, withdraw from the navy (except to stay in the Navy Reserve), and begin his graduate work at the University of Wisconsin. Carolyn stayed on to finish work for a bachelor's degree at UC Berkeley. "We promised to write letters to keep in touch—and this we did," Carolyn recalls.

Their courtship progressed through weekly letters that exposed common interests, dreams, and a playful spirit. "The Christmas Howard was in Madison and I was in Berkeley, we were writing letters back and forth. [One time] I sent him a wool dress sock filled with a few little items, including some new pictures of me. In it I wrote a note, 'If you want The Mate, you must come to California for it.' I don't know if I was clever or desperate, but it worked! He came."

More months of separation and study followed, and their correspondence turned to spiritual things. Recalls Carolyn, "During that year apart I sent him the C. S. Lewis book *Beyond Personality,* which I was thrilled with, and he responded enthusiastically. That little book later became part of *Mere Christianity,* along with two other small books, *The Case for Christianity* and *Christian Behavior.*" Far more than exchanging "sweet nothings," the two were discovering intellectual and spiritual interests that would be a strong foundation for a lifetime together.

Carolyn picks up the story: "In June 1947 Howard and a friend, Ali Dad Farmanfarma, drove out to California ostensibly to see the sights. Ali Dad was one of the princes of Iran and was attending the University of Wisconsin. By August, Howard and I were convinced we were meant to marry, although circumstances were making it hard for us to plan a wedding. So we decided to put a wedding together in five days. It grew beyond our intentions—but it was never in our minds that we should have waited. Ali Dad was best man." Howard's family in Wisconsin was understandably surprised that this Midwest boy returned home already hitched up with a California girl.

Howard rode the two thousand miles back to Madison alone to find housing for his new bride. With housing at a premium everywhere, he was only able to find a room. Carolyn followed a few weeks later by plane, her first commercial plane trip. In her words, "Those seventeen days were some of the longest I ever endured. After that, if we could only be together, any room in Madison was good enough." They later moved to another room, then finally to a small apartment.

At the University of Wisconsin, Howard soon distinguished himself by applying his experience in radio frequency (RF) communications to his first love—chemistry. He believed the new wartime technologies could dramatically improve laboratory instrumentation, producing more precise results with less tedious analysis. Under the research direction of Professor W. J. Blaedel, Howard worked on his first graduate-level paper titled "High Frequency Titrations: A Study of Instruments." Titrations and Instrumentation later became the focus of his PhD thesis and a number of papers from that era of his life.

Titration is a process for measuring the amount of a selected chemical in, for example, blood. The basic idea is to cause a reaction during which that chemical is used up. The standard way to cause such a reaction is to add "reagent" into the solution, observing exactly when the chemical is used up and how much reagent was used in the process. This "end point" can be recognized as a change in color, voltage, or some other indicator.

During typical chemistry experiments of the 1940s, multiple steps with multiple reagents were required to reach an observable end point, and the complexity of steps in the process allowed for appreciable error to creep into the experiments. Fresh from radar school, Howard began sending high-frequency signals through the sample solutions and measuring the changes in high-frequency conductivity caused by adding the reagent to the solution. His work led to a process that was both easier and more precise. One of Howard's lifelong passions was looking for ways to remove tedium from the work of analytical chemistry, automating wherever possible and always looking to take advantage of the latest technology breakthroughs. If no breakthroughs were available, he saw it as an opportunity to create one.

As Stan Crouch, his PhD student and longtime colleague and friend describes it, Howard "legitimized the study of instrumentation. Before Howard, those who designed, tested, and applied instruments were often thought of as 'gadgeteers' and not true scientists. Howard's work changed all that."

It was also time for breakthroughs on the home front. The Malmstadts' first child—daughter Cynthia—arrived in January 1949. In Carolyn's words: "Howard was one of the few men I have known, maybe the only one, who was not put off by the strangeness of most newborns. He immediately bonded with his little girl, totally optimistic about her eventual good looks. We soon had an adorable baby."

Having received his MS in 1949 and PhD in 1950 at Wisconsin, Howard continued on there as a postdoctoral associate. His second daughter, Alice, arrived in 1951, and Howard knew he had to find a job to support his growing family. Soon thereafter he accepted a position as instructor at the University of Illinois (U of I) at Urbana-Champaign. His contributions to academia and the field of chemistry were about to soar to new heights.

3.

The Chemistry of Teamwork

*Jazz-band leaders know how to integrate the "voices" in the band
without diminishing their uniqueness. The individuals in the
band are expected to play solo and together.*

—MAX DE PREE

*Howard's research team was gathered around tables in a motel, of all
places, after a long brainstorming session in the lab. The other team
members were enjoying pizza, beer, and card playing. Apart from the
pizza, these activities would normally drive Howard to distraction, but
there was a problem to solve. It was a mark of his character and his commitment to teamwork that he was in the thick of the event anyway, very
much present and affirming the people on the team. By the end of the night,
the team got the breakthrough they were seeking.*

Howard Malmstadt accomplished many things as an individual, but his proudest achievements were with others as part of a
team. As a young professor, he learned to function in teams, and
because of his collaborative spirit, he was given increasing authority to lead laboratory research groups.

Though his career at U of I would span twenty-seven years, it
started with more struggle than success. For the first few years, the
family survived on an annual salary under four thousand dollars. In
the "publish or perish" world of academia, his initially low output

was viewed askance by the department. Fortunately, several older colleagues stood up for him, advising the others to give him time. For Howard's part, he worked hard in establishing his teaching, as well as perfecting his research prior to publishing. His first published work at U of I was titled "Automatic Spectrophotometric Titrations" and came out in 1954.

That same year he was promoted to assistant professor. The new job security prompted Howard and Carolyn to take the plunge into home ownership. They had just spent a happy two and a half years in army barracks that had been converted into three-room units for returning GIs to use in transition to education or jobs. Having two little girls, they fit right into this neighborhood full of families with children. However, things got a little more crowded when Jonathan Howard came along. With borrowed money, the Malmstadts scraped together the down payment for a National Homes prefab in Urbana and moved across town six months later. Four and a half years after this, Howard convinced Carolyn that they should arrange for a new home to be built to their specifications, conveniently located close to all the schools, including the university. That would be their family home for the next twenty years.

The new home and other benefits were made possible by salary increases resulting from Howard's promotions and research work. By the end of the 1950s he had been promoted through associate professor to a full professor of chemistry.

Dr. Malmstadt was poised to take his place in the "family tree" of chemistry innovators, which was rooted in the likes of Louis Nicolas Vauquelin, an outstanding organic chemist and professor; Joseph Louis Gay-Lussac, a pioneer in the study of the thermal expansion properties of gases and in experimentation techniques; and Justus von Liebig, the first to be credited with creating a practical chemical teaching laboratory.

From his earliest years at U of I, Howard was always seeking ways to make chemistry education practical and more accessible to people in academia, industry, and government. He relentlessly explored new ways to improve titration techniques. As described earlier, in high-school chemistry classes, titration usually involves adding a "reagent" chemical to a solution containing an unknown amount of a chemical until the solution changes color. The amount of reagent needed to get to that point helps to determine how much of a particular chemical is present in the solution. Another approach is to measure the electrical qualities of the solution as reagent is added.

Howard's contribution was to automate this process using an electrical circuit that would sense when to shut off reagent delivery to the solution when the end point is reached. This titrator was later produced commercially by E. H. Sargent & Co. as the Sargent-Malmstadt Spectro/Electro Titrator.

This device was one of the first successful automated instruments ever sold—a pioneering work that blended chemistry, electronics, and instrumentation. In a not-so-subtle dig at previous attempts, the Sargent catalog entry proclaims "Greater operational savings than any former so-called automatic equipment." We have no record of the negotiations that resulted in this choice of words. One can only imagine Howard cringing at that dismissive and condescending tone. More in keeping with his own thinking and actions through the years were these words from the same catalog entry: "Correct end point is automatically derived by the circuit— no statistical or theoretical studies needed. No presetting of voltages. Push-button start, automatic shutoff."

With Jim Winefordner, one of his early PhD students, Howard pioneered a more accurate measuring method called precision null-point potentiometry. This approach involves comparing electrical potentials by using electrodes to make a "battery" with two solutions containing the same chemical. One solution has a known amount of the chemical, and the other one an unknown amount. By using the basic principle of a two-pan balance, the amount of chemical in the known solution is varied until the battery potential (voltage) goes to zero. At this null point, the two solutions have the same amount of the chemical being measured; the two pans are "balanced."

Dr. Malmstadt exhibited an extraordinary gift for taking detailed insights from his research and integrating them with other concepts and technologies toward a focused goal. Having achieved the goal, he wanted to make it easier for others to follow in his footsteps. But his own footsteps moved forward at a relentless pace, continually breaking new ground in multiple areas in the fast-growing field of analytical chemistry. That pace earned him the nickname "H-nu," which is the energy of the photon, a packet of light—and a play on his initials HV.

Howard and U of I student Phil Hicks (later a PhD student under Howard's friend Dr. Blaedel at Wisconsin) also pioneered an "initial rate method" in kinetic analysis. In a paper published in 1960, they described a system for determining glucose levels in blood serum. Their key concept was that the rate over the first few seconds of a chemical reaction was directly related to the concentrations of the reactants in the solution. This discovery meant that it was not necessary to wait for the "end point." Instead, the early portion of the reaction would provide enough data to indicate the desired answer, thus saving time and reducing the potential for errors. This method later became standard practice in both analytical and clinical chemistry. Today, one can find this principle used in portable blood-sugar monitors and modern digital thermometers, which don't have to wait for the thermometer to get to the final temperature. Howard subsequently was honored at the International Symposium on Kinetics in Analytical Chemistry as one of the two pioneers of this revolutionary laboratory method.

Kinetic methods led Howard to become interested in other clinical applications for chemical analysis. He often latched on to new discoveries by others, foreseeing the potential directions that others' research could take. A classic example of this is atomic absorption (AA), a technique first presented almost simultaneously in 1955 by Sir Alan Walsh of Australia and by Dutch scientists C. Th. J. Alkemade and J. M. W. Milatz as having possibilities for analysis of elements.[1] The atomic absorption technique involves vaporizing liquids or solids in a flame, then passing light through the flame and measuring the effect those atoms have on the light, called "attenuation." The effect on different colors (wavelengths) has a pattern that shows how much of a given chemical was sprayed into the flame. The device that measures these effects across the color spectrum is called a "spectrometer."

Picking up on this work and applying what he had developed earlier comparing electrical potential (voltages), Howard introduced the technique of precision null-point atomic absorption spectrochemical analysis in a 1960 paper with W. E. Chambers, who a year earlier had received his PhD while studying under Howard. This paper introduced the famous f-equation, which became a familiar sight to many Malmstadt students. This equation relates the signal in atomic absorption (and emission) to the concentration of the solution being analyzed. Once again, this is much like using a two-pan scale to measure something unknown using something known by making them balance.

Howard's papers were almost always coauthored with his students. He practiced teamwork, not settling for only believing in it abstractly. The breakthroughs he and others achieved were directly tied to the synergy of the various teams he formed.

As Howard's research began attracting worldwide attention, new opportunities opened to him. In late 1959 he began a sabbatical year and soon thereafter was named a Guggenheim Fellow. Funds from this prestigious award allowed him to travel with his family to several labs in the United States and Europe, principally in Holland and Switzerland. In Holland he visited the Rijksuniversiteit Utrecht where he met with Professor Alkamede, the pioneer of atomic absorption technology. Howard came back energized with new ideas and soon began applying them in his lab at U of I, Urbana-Champaign.

Also generating excitement and new ideas in Howard's lab was the escalating space race between the United States and the Soviet Union. In 1958, the U.S. Congress passed legislation to create the National Aeronautics and Space Administration (NASA). University, government, and business labs were joining forces to try to advance America's space technology. Howard was well positioned to provide leadership for this new wave of research and development. The urgency of the space race convinced Howard even more of the necessity of scientists' knowing and using electronics and of the importance of instrumentation, including miniaturization. U of I research sparked new advances in space technology and job opportunities for Howard's graduate students in the new agency. Indeed, some of Howard's first- and second-generation students are working at NASA today.

Howard would later become motivated by a pressing problem right here on earth: clean drinking water. That challenge would require all the training of his instrumentation work and team-building experience.

In 1963 the American Chemical Society (ACS) honored Howard Malmstadt with its Analytical Division Award for Chemical Instrumentation. This award was the first in a long string of scientific awards he would receive over his lifetime. The ACS award specifically honors scientists who have designed and created instruments that have "made a significant impact on the field," "demonstrated innovative use" in doing chemical measurement, stimulated like research by others, and authored papers and books that have had an "influential role" in encouraging the use of chemical instrumentation.

Howard Malmstadt's work fit all of these criteria, and his vision passed to his students. The ACS Award was subsequently received by an impressive array of "Malmstadters": Chris Enke (1974), Jim Winefordner (1978), John Walters (1979), Harry Pardue (1982), Gary Hieftje (1985), Bonner Denton (1989), Stan Crouch (2001), and second-generation offspring Jonathan Sweedler (2002, PhD under Denton) and J. Michael Ramsey (2003, PhD under Hieftje).

Howard's training and early work in electrochemistry in the U of I Chemistry Department created the potential for conflict with the head of the analytical division, Dr. Herbert A. Laitinen, himself an established electrochemist. This could have sparked a bitter intradepartmental rivalry. But in typical fashion, Howard responded to this new "boulder in the stream" by shifting his own research from titrations to a new field called atomic spectroscopy, including the atomic absorption process described above. He pursued this new area of study by spending his summers visiting industrial and academic spectroscopic laboratories.

A subsequent U of I paper with university colleague R. G. Scholz on another branch of atomic spectroscopy called emission spectroscopy ("Emission Spectrochemical Analysis of Vanadium and Iron in Titanium Tetrachloride") illustrates his trademark passions by describing a process that is "rapid, inexpensive, [and] accurate," with "possible general application." The process described in this paper, called the spark-in-spray excitation method, uses the same principle as a perfume atomizer, using high-voltage electricity to create a color spectrum that reveals the concentrations of certain elements—in this case vanadium and iron.

Howard continued to refine this process with PhD students John Walters, Ray Barnes, and Ed Piepmeier. Their work in spark-source excitation increased understanding of spark discharges, which are widely used today in emission spectroscopy and mass spectrometry. According to the American Society for Mass Spectrometry, "Mass spectrometry is a powerful analytical technique that is used to identify unknown compounds, to quantify known compounds, and to elucidate the structure and chemical properties of molecules."[2]

As Winefordner and many others of Howard's students and coworkers have attested, Howard's belief in them and passionate interest in the science they were exploring led his teams to accomplish far more than the individual team members would have on their own. Howard set high standards for himself, and the power of that modeling caused those around him to rise to higher standards in their own professional and personal lives. In Winefordner's words: "Every time I came out of his office I was more upbeat than when I went in."

In 1964, no doubt in response to the increasing demands of academic life, Howard and Carolyn began a search for a summer getaway and found it along Lake Michigan. As Carolyn puts it, "It was another one of those times when we were sure God led us right to what He wanted us to have." This peaceful and beautiful lakeside home continues to be Carolyn's year-round residence. Not only was it a haven for Howard, away from the stress of his research and teaching work, but it was also a place of hospitality. Over the years, Howard and Carolyn hosted numerous book-writing sessions, research-group meetings, and social events at their wooded hideaway.

Between 1964 and 1967 Howard assembled a team to develop a monochromator for the Heath Company. A monochromator is an instrument that can isolate specific wavelengths (colors) of light. It was to become the central part in a complete system for molecular and atomic spectrophotometric analysis. This system is used today in a wide range of applications, such as determining the quality of drinking water and for blood tests to help diagnose medical problems.

Howard's visions for the monochromator led him to set tough standards for his team: the instrument's cost needed to be under a thousand dollars; the unit must be shippable, with no damage in transit; no field engineer should be required to install or fine-tune it on delivery; the resolution should be one angstrom or better (a measure of the degree of isolating wavelengths).

Howard's U of I research and production team included John Walters as technical lead, Jack Haynes as engineering lead, Neil Shimp as production lead, Chris Enke as electronic consultant, Wayne Kooy as engineering consultant, and Ray Vogel on performance evaluation.

As John Walters would comment later: "In almost all situations, we almost all wanted to please him. He could make what seemed to be outrageous statements in our group meetings, leaving us grinding our teeth, but somehow we would just blast or grind away until we either met those expectations or came as close as we could, given our abilities and situations."

From a technical standpoint, the mechanisms for setting and preserving the alignment before and during shipping were built into the design, which included innovative contributions from Jack Haynes and Chris Enke.

Howard's book *Courageous Leaders Transforming Their World,* which he coauthored in 1999 with James Halcomb and David Hamilton, says: "Team unity requires leaders who are effective communicators and are committed to a common goal."[3] Howard modeled this with the monochromator team (and many others), which is why they so often met his lofty objectives. Howard kept them focused and productive toward the goal. He assembled his research teams based on the individuals' particular strengths and made sure each member believed he could meet or exceed the team's goals. Howard worked hard to ensure that the natural tension of different perspectives and approaches led to innovation, not unproductive dissension. Under his leadership, there was no reason for individual egos to get in the way. As John Walters summarizes: "In all the years following my time at U of I, I never had as much excitement, fun, and delight in discovery as I did while I was with Howard."

Howard and those working with him kept viewing the possibilities for spectrochemical analysis from different angles, much as a jeweler admires the many facets of a diamond. He worked with Gary Hieftje on what is known as flame emission spectroscopy. Together with Jim Winefordner, Bonner Denton, and Emil Cordos he pushed the frontiers of spectroscopy by introducing new and more accurate methods.

These breakthroughs in molecular and atomic spectroscopy spurred Howard toward wider clinical applications for his work. What delighted him most was knowing that his teams' research had broad application in medicine, industry, aerospace technology, and other fields. One of the hallmarks of Howard Malmstadt's life was his desire to develop technology that could be used to help people in their daily lives. In that season of nonstop advances he was soon handed a tool that would take his research to new heights.

Dr. Larry Faulkner, former head of the U of I Chemistry Department and currently president of the University of Texas, said, "Howard Malmstadt was at least a decade ahead of others in understanding the great qualitative changes that could occur in analytical chemistry by taking advantage, first, of the advances in microelectronics and, later, by the new technology resting on microprocessors."

Microcomputers became a central part of Howard's thinking in the mid-1960s, when he visited Harley Ross at Oak Ridge National Laboratories. When he returned to U of I, he exhorted his students to "think digital." Again, the river of Howard's life flowed smoothly around the "boulder" of this new technology, digging a deep and wide channel for him and those working with him. One of the many applications he foresaw for this new technology was counting. For example, he quickly recognized that counting photons was a far more accurate spectroscopy method than the classic analog light measurements. One of his simple but powerful insights with respect to counting was that it needs to take place within certain boundaries. It's one thing to measure how many events occur; it is far more meaningful to note how many events take place in a certain unit of time.

In our day of rapidly falling prices for home computers, it is hard to imagine life without microcomputers. But Howard and his protégés were in the forefront of building and using minicomputers and, later, microcomputers not only to measure data but also as an integrated part of instrumentation, allowing experiments to be controlled by computer programs.

Howard became the owner of a personal computer (PC) in 1984 after a few students heard his comment about wanting one and twenty-eight of them pitched in together to buy it. Ironically, Howard was slow in adapting to PCs, preferring to handwrite and depend on others to transcribe his writings to the computer. As software became easier to use over the years, Howard gradually became a computer user, but the curious fact remains that he typically lagged behind those he worked with in terms of PC proficiency.

The full impact of Howard Malmstadt's research may never be known, but his peers in the fields of analytical chemistry and spectroscopy have recognized him as one of most influential scientists and educators of our time. In 1995—years after he had left active laboratory research—Howard was summoned to the Pittcon event in New Orleans where he received the Maurice F. Hasler Award for achievement in spectroscopy.

Brian R. Strohmeier, chairman of the Hasler Award committee, stated:

Professor Malmstadt made immense contributions to analytical chemistry, especially in the areas of atomic and molecular spectroscopy, both as an educator and a researcher ... he is well known for his brilliant scientific intellect, nurturing personality, high moral standards, enthusiasm, creativity, and leadership in analytical chemistry. The world of atomic spectroscopy today is largely a result of the many generations of students that he has mentored.

Perhaps no laboratory environment in recent history was such a fertile field for creativity and discovery as Dr. Howard Malmstadt's at the U of I, Urbana-Champaign. For research grants, awards, fellowships, patents, and the overall impact of their work, the Malmstadt groups' academic and scientific legacy may be unequaled. What was it about Howard Malmstadt that enabled him to draw out so much potential from his students? What teaching principles and philosophies did he apply that fostered such excellence? And what was it about these teams that made them so productive, mutually affirming, and personally close even many years later?

4.

A Passion for Teaching

A teacher affects eternity; he can never tell where his influence stops.

—HENRY ADAMS

Gary Hieftje, one of Howard's PhD students, was pushing a cart along a hallway at the U of I. The cart—dubbed the "voltswagon"—rattled along under the burden of a daisy chain of one hundred ninety-volt batteries. Hieftje reflected proudly on how he had met Howard's challenge to come up with a high-voltage source. Suddenly, the whole thing fell onto the floor and was smashed to smithereens. Ed Piepmeier, another Malmstadt student who witnessed the incident, commented wryly that he hoped nothing was ruined. Gary thought his academic career might be, but not so. Howard kept encouraging Gary as his career moved far beyond this little incident.

Over the course of Howard Malmstadt's career at U of I, he mentored sixty-four PhD students. Although a large number, it is by no means a record for analytical-chemistry professors. What most multiplied Howard's influence was the fact that many of his students took posts in academia and went on to have PhD students of their own. In fact, there are third-, fourth-, and even fifth-generation Malmstadt students making contributions to analytical chemistry today and winning more than their share of grants and professional awards.

What accounts for such a rich legacy of lives dedicated to promoting analytical chemistry in the halls and labs of universities,
industry, and government? One oft-repeated answer from former
students is Howard's great enthusiasm for science in general and
analytical chemistry in particular with its full range of challenge
and opportunity. His persistent optimism, his love for his teaching, and his passion for discovery affected everyone who came in
contact with him.

One of these was John Walters, a PhD student under Howard
in 1964. "Howard did not pit those of us in his research group
against each other," Walters said in an Honor's Day address at St.
Olaf College. Howard Malmstadt's students worked in teams,
with unique teaching assignments and responsibilities, Walters
said. "We combined our unique talents to make his graduate
course truly excellent. And we loved it. We had our egos. We had
our moments. But, there was no attempt to homogenize us into a
palatable blend. That was what made the whole thing work."

The challenge of Howard's running a research group with fifteen graduate students and three postdocs, teaching a graduate
class and lab, writing three books, and developing a new field of
electronics in chemistry required bold leadership. This leadership
"came in persuading us to 'buy into' the effort, that it was worth
doing, and that it was our unique talents that would combine to
solve the problem," Walters says.

Walters commented that a friend had once said, "When there
is trouble in the class, I always look to the front of the room."
When Walters was under Howard's leadership, "things were good
'at the front of the room.' It made a huge difference."[1]

Howard's belief in teamwork and the "immersion" style of
learning had emerged from his experience at the MIT Radiation
Laboratory. The first opportunity Howard had to fully apply this
immersion concept was in the development of what became known
as the U of I Summer Course on Electronics. Initially, Howard
worked with one of Dr. Laitinen's research students—a promising
electrochemist named Chris Enke—to develop an electronics course
at U of I. Based on that course, Howard applied to the National
Science Foundation (NSF) to fund a three-week electronics course

accessible to scientists from academia, industry, and government. The challenge was to compress a semester's worth of material into three weeks so the course could be offered during the summer break.

The next challenge for this course was to provide each student with flexible work stations. At the time, the state of the art was the "job board," which was essentially a fixed design whereby the student would "connect the dots" with wires. Once the connections were made and soldered, the job board's useful life was over. Mulling over this problem, Howard and Chris came up with an innovation: spring clips. This design allowed for connections to be made in the course of an experiment, then quickly and easily dismantled at the end of the day, ready to make new connections for a different experiment the next day.

Although Howard missed the first instance of the new course (being on sabbatical), he made his mark on its form. The students spent long hours in a mix of lectures, demos, and—most important—hands-on experiments. It was an intensive three-week experience in which the students got to know one another and absorbed larger quantities of material at the same time. When everyone retired to a local pub to relax in the evenings, the conversations revolved around the electronics they were learning.

As hoped for, the course appealed to scientists from beyond the walls of U of I. In fact, on one occasion some musicians joined the course so they could incorporate electronics into their craft. For more than a decade, this course enlightened thousands of scientists to the potential applications of electronics in their research. During that time, Howard and Chris published a book called *Electronics for Scientists,* which served as a framework for the "Summer Course." As always, Howard wanted readers to be able to apply the information, so he insisted that the book include a work-station kit with essentials for a variety of experiments.

The course content was literally spreading around the world as professors and scientists from various countries returned home and taught electronics based on the book and the Heath Company work-stations kit. In the late 1970s, the American Chemistry Society approached Howard about creating a two- or three-day version of the Summer Course that could be taken on the road. This shorter, mobile format would allow far more people from industry and government labs to participate.

Howard relished the challenge of taking his teaching to such a broad audience. He and Chris, together with Stan Crouch, who earned his PhD under Howard in 1967, teamed up to condense three weeks of teaching down to two days. Later, a third day was added because of pressure from students for more lab time. In creating the course, the trio discovered how well their creative giftings complemented one another's—Howard the visionary, Chris the idea factory, and Stan the implementer. From this relationship emerged a mutual respect and productive synergy that grew ever stronger through the years.

During the first instance of this road course, in 1979 at the Eastern Analytical Symposium in New York City, the team realized they needed to get away from the lecture/demo model and introduce the hands-on training model that Howard insisted on. In accomplishing this, they created an updated "lab kit" that was flexible, inexpensive, and portable.

This "short course," as the Malmstadt people came to know it, became a well-recognized fixture on the teaching circuit. Over the following years it was taught more than seventy times, at numerous scientific conferences and even at such research labs as AT&T Bell Labs (later to become part of Lucent Technologies, Inc.). Even after Howard left U of I in the early 1980s, he continued to deliver the course, constantly improving teaching methods and course content.

Part of Howard Malmstadt's brilliance as a teacher was his ability to simplify complex issues and impart them in such a way that students could not only understand the concepts but also teach them to others.

Alex Scheeline, a second-generation Malmstadter, describes his first teaching experience under Howard at a chemistry symposium:

I can't remember a single slide of Howard's, only that he had an aura about him, that he had a command of so much information while at the same time being so genuinely concerned and involved with everyone he met that he fairly radiated. He made everything seem simple without being simplistic. He attracted a mob of people who wanted to talk with him. Stan Crouch [Alex's mentor] introduced me as would a proud father. Howard warmly responded, then moved on to more pressing and substantive discussions. This, in retrospect, was the beginning of what I reported in another story: budgeting time in proportion to importance and demand, but always making each person feel important.

Howard and his team met hundreds of scientists in their global rounds teaching the "short course." The students represented fields as diverse as medicine, atomic energy, astronomy, engineering, physics, and more. The "short course" team successfully demonstrated to them how scientific instrumentation could enhance their research and achieve breakthroughs in their various fields. Stan Crouch catalogued the course's impact and found that scientists who took it better understood the capabilities of scientific instrumentation and thus could make more effective use of it, were equipped to design new instruments or improve existing ones, and were able to troubleshoot instruments to reduce downtime and to communicate more effectively with repair technicians. Furthermore, they had increased confidence in measurements. The "short course" ensured that instrumentation became part of standard undergraduate textbooks and lab assignments.

In 1984, the American Chemical Society honored Howard for his contributions to the teaching of electronics for analytical chemistry. He received the ACS Analytical Division Award for Excellence in Teaching. The list of the criteria for this award matches Howard's career remarkably well:ß

1. Authorship of an influential textbook for an analytical chemistry course (*Howard wrote thirteen influential textbooks over the course of his career.*)

2. Design and implementation of a successful new approach to teaching analytical chemistry *(His immersion teaching and hands-on focus became benchmarks of the academic world in that field.)*

3. Stimulation through teaching or research mentorship of a significant number of students to become analytical chemists *(sixty-four PhD students, most of whom became analytical chemists).*

4. Development and publishing of innovative experiments *(Automation of titration is an early example.)*

5. Design of improved equipment for teaching labs *(the kits!)*

6. Publication of widely quoted articles on teaching analytical chemistry *(Howard authored/coauthored over 150 articles).*

Howard's students followed in his footsteps to win this award too—John Walters in 1984, Jim Winefordner in 1995, Stan Crouch in 1996, and Gary Hieftje in 1998. His colleague Chris Enke received this award in 2003. As often as possible, Howard made a point of being at the presentation to encourage his academic "children."

In the midst of training the waves of students over the years, Howard's teacher's heart influenced his own family. His daughter Alice writes:

> Another of the most significant influences my dad had on me was when I was a college freshman. I was about two-thirds into the semester and was struggling with a biology lab class and failing a statistics class. I don't remember if I called my parents or wrote telling them I was…just not making it. I told them I was a failure and knew I had let them down. I didn't know what they wanted me to do— quit now and save money? I wondered what I would do, since it was obvious a college degree was no longer an option. My dreams of becoming a teacher or anything worthwhile faded before me.
>
> About four days later I received a [hand-written] letter from my dad. The gist was this: it takes a lot more than a difficult class and a failing grade to become a failure. He told me that even though I didn't think I

could accomplish my goal, he had faith in me. He knew I could do it. But if for some reason, after giving it my best, I didn't make it, there would be a better plan for me. That has come back to me over and over through life as my personal relationship with the Lord grows. Just like the Father in heaven who gives us the freedom to fail and come back to Him for direction, my dad pointed the way for me to accept myself as God made me and not to expect too much, but never to accept too little either. "With God all things are possible."

Amid the campus disillusionment of the 1960s, Howard was a professor students could talk to about the troubling issues of the times—the Vietnam War and the Kennedy and King assassinations. These events caused many university students to doubt the validity of America's basic institutions and basic assumptions underlying the culture. Howard, as a staunch Republican, was not pleased by his perception that the Democratic Johnson administration was preventing the military from winning the Vietnam War. Nevertheless, he refused to succumb to discouragement or to approve the tactics of student activists or draft dodgers who fled to Canada. Throughout that challenging time, Howard's life modeled to students persistent hope and perseverance.

Howard was happiest when surrounded by students and coworkers in a teamwork context, whether blueskying new ways that their research could be used or brainstorming a solution for the latest technical challenge. One example was during development of the Heath monochromator. Howard was struggling with a design challenge: they needed a solution for resynchronizing the stepper motors between the chart recorder and the monochromator wavelength drive after the monochromator had been switched in and out of its fast-scan mode.

One long evening was devoted to a superbrainstorming session on the problem, then the team retired to a local motel for pizza, beer, and card playing. From that session emerged the breakthrough idea; someone picked up two poker chips and rotated them in opposite directions against each other; suddenly the team had their solution for the slow-scan, stepper-motor drive clutch.

Howard set standards for team research that profoundly influenced many research environments around the world. In a field where a dictator approach is too often the norm, he believed strongly in consensus, the dignity of each individual, and the urgency of integrating each one's gifts fully into the effort. Each team member was expected to take on his share of the responsibility for the team's actions and be motivated by the challenge before the team. An important ingredient of his teams was freedom to follow ideas where they led; if the result was a dead end, so be it—but just maybe it would lead to new discoveries.

Where others might create a culture dominated by fear of failure and enforced by angry shouting and intimidation, Howard cultivated high expectations but was gracious to others when things didn't turn out well. His students and all who worked with him speak of trying hard to avoid not his anger but rather his disappointment. Often that would be expressed through his silence rather than words. This approach meant that some would be left wondering what his true feelings were about their performance.

Willard Harrison, one of Howard's PhD students, tells of working with a brand-new Westinghouse hollow cathode lamp under Howard's direction. Unfortunately, in testing this state-of-the-art product, Willard failed to see a decimal point when reading the specifications, which called for a maximum current of five milliamps. Instead, Willard applied fifty milliamps, or ten times the rated maximum. For a brief time, the lamp burned very brightly indeed—then shorted out. Willard, seeing his dismal future academic career pass before his eyes, rushed the stricken lamp to the glass shop, where he had it cut open, unshorted the lamp, and installed a gas valve. "I then took the pathetic carcass meekly to Howard, pointing out that I had stumbled onto a new invention: a reconstructable hollow cathode lamp, which in fact wasn't invented for another five years. Howard was not amused, but he did extend forgiveness." One bright side to the story is that the incident led Dr. Harrison to devote much of his lifetime of research to similar discharge devices.

John Walters describes this characteristic as "enabling and ennobling. He made you want to reach into your soul, do better, improve your results." As Howard himself commented, taking a personal interest increased a person's learning potential.

Howard took fatherly delight in all his PhD students' discoveries and achievements. Always approachable, he gave counsel to those who sought him out, long after they had left his classroom.

Former students who were interviewed for this book expressed in various ways that they "felt privileged" to have learned directly from Dr. Howard Malmstadt. To them he demonstrated that extraordinary combination of humanity, academic brilliance, passion for learning, love for his field, and devotion to his students that typify a truly great teacher.

5.

The Pursuit of Excellence

*Courageous leaders who seek to transform their world accept chal-
lenges beyond their capacity. They aim for a goal that requires
resources above and beyond themselves.*
    —FROM *Courageous Leaders Transforming Their World*

*E*xcellence and elegance. These qualities permeated the life work of
*Howard Malmstadt. From professional pursuits such as research and
teaching to personal pursuits such as family life and church work, he continually set high standards for himself and others.*

Nevertheless, Howard's fearless quest for excellence sometimes
got him into a bit of trouble. John Walters recalls how devoted
Howard was to making sure every student understood the instruments well enough to teach them to others. In one case, there was
an arc/spark source in the 421 emission lab that was a key compo-
nent of the first few experiments. It had to be mechanically phased
just so to work right, and almost everyone using it was frightened
by its cable-raising power. When used in the arc mode, it was
indeed both lethal and frightening. John was afraid to open the
side panel to show his lab section how the huge mercury arc rectifiers worked, and told Howard so. John remembers Howard saying something like, "Oh, that's nothing to be afraid of. Here, let
me show you where the connection is for these rectifiers." Howard

then reached into the running source to point at a wire. Just as
John was turning around to look inside, Howard came flying
backward out of the source, about a foot off the ground, loudly
proclaiming the only blue word that John ever heard him say.
Upon regaining his composure and his footing, Howard agreed
that it might be better to cut a Plexiglas window into the side
panel and just have people look but not touch when the source
was running. In truth, there were few limits to Howard's desire to
teach and help others learn, other than, perhaps, a fully charged
(600 volts) capacitor. John will always remember Howard for this
desire to do the right things and do them well.

Howard recognized that to truly learn a subject, one must
move from a simple understanding to an appreciation of its most
complex details. He called this "grasping its elegance." Those who
grasp the elegance are usually most able to communicate the subject to others, and Howard modeled this over and over. He encouraged countless others to persist until they reached elegance in their
understanding as well.

In *Courageous Leaders Transforming Their World,* Howard
describes "buoyant tenacity" as a hallmark of leadership that excels.
Some may associate such tenacity with inflexibility, but this bull-
dog mentality bears no resemblance to pigheaded stubbornness.
"The difference lies in the courageous leader's ability to distinguish between the Desired End Items and Overall Objective on
one hand and the means of achieving them on the other. Chang-
ing circumstances...may require creative modifications...The
courageous leader adjusts the strategies to lay hold unwaveringly
to the unchanging Overall Objective."[1]

A fairly abstract example of this flexibility dealt with the policy question of accepting government money for research work.
In his early U of I years, Howard tried to stay independent of fed-
eral funding. He believed this would keep his teams focused on
pursuing research where it led them rather than where the funding directed them. It also had the effect of keeping the research
teams consistently poor. From Howard's perspective, this self-
enforced austerity made the teams more creative.

For Howard himself, this was good preparation for a time to come when he and all those around him would become volunteers with no salary or research funding to rely on.

In the 1970s, however, Howard agreed to serve on the National Institutes of Health study panel helping to evaluate grant proposals. At a time when his work was taking him in the direction of clinical chemistry, this experience opened his eyes to the potential that grant money held for enabling bigger and better-equipped teams, thus resulting in more quality research. Even as his strategy for "funding the party" changed, his goal remained the same: assemble high-quality teams that could accomplish far more together than as individuals.

Gary Hieftje, who teamed with Howard several times, describes his mentor's passionate focus on the ideal. "By definition, the ideal should be unattainable, keeping it beyond the team's achievements at any point in time. It should be an unchanging goal, against which any proposed solution can be measured. As the shortcomings of the current proposed solution become clear, hopefully a productive path for bringing it closer to the ideal will become clear as well." Dr. Hieftje's first challenge from Howard was to find an ideal spark source. His pursuit of the ideal solution took him on a lifetime journey of discovery. "The more I worked with Howard on other challenges, the more I saw the benefits of his philosophy of holding out an ideal as a goal for the individual or team."

Howard's pursuit of excellence did not go unnoticed by his fellow scientists. In 1978, he received the Outstanding Analytical Chemist Award from the Society for Analytical Chemists of Pittsburgh. This award honored "Professor Malmstadt for his many achievements in the field of analytical instrumentation and his impact on the education of analytical chemists." In fact, the award was created for the purpose of honoring Dr. Malmstadt as its first recipient. Then in 1987 the Federation of Analytical Chemists and Spectroscopy Societies (FACSS) awarded Howard the Anachem Award for "outstanding research contributions and service to the field of analytical chemistry."

Howard's passion for excellence extended to his role as a parent. Alice, his second daughter, relates the following story that illustrates his interest in his children and in the excellence of their education:

> While I was in junior high, one of my English assignments was to write directions on how to run a piece of equipment in our school, such as the film projector, slide projector, sewing machine, and so forth so that anyone who could read would be able to run it. My English teacher had lectured us about the two most important criteria for writing directions: write clearly so there could be no errors if followed correctly, and use as few words as possible. Every day Dad would ask me, "How are you doing?" and then follow it up with "What did you learn today?" or "What's new at school?" When I told him the assignment, he became very enthusiastic as though this was one of the smartest assignments ever given in junior high. He proceeded to tell me how important it was to be able to write clearly and concisely. He said that too many people spend pages and pages explaining what they could describe in a few. He believed this so strongly that he ended up calling my English teacher and complimenting her on the assignment, encouraging her to have her students practice more of this type of critical, informative writing. This had a great impact on me at the time. I never forgot it.

Howard considered writing to be a key tool for his students. He modeled this emphasis by coauthoring dozens of articles and books. One of his coauthors describes the process:

> Throughout this collaborative writing effort, several procedures evolved, made possible by Howard's inherent selflessness and inclusiveness. Individual authors had primary responsibility for certain chapters, but all chapters became collaborative efforts. One did not offer suggestions for

changes in another's chapter; one wrote out whatever he thought would work better. One did not argue for one's original version, but accepted that a suggested rewrite indicated that work was needed in that section. We came to welcome each other's revisions; it became apparent that through these exchanges, the chapters were much more readable and the book was more consistent in style. We would brainstorm for hours over outlines and approach, always seeking that "essence" that would become the main concept of a chapter or section.[2]

"Through this experience, Stan Crouch and I came to regard effective writing as an essential skill for a scientist and used these same procedures when working with our own students," Chris Enke says. "Hours were spent on just coming up with a title for a paper."

Some of Howard's U of I colleagues came to view him as a tinkerer rather than a true scientist, because of his fascination with perfecting instruments. They were certainly correct in pointing out Howard's constant prodding of his students to get the job done right. "Good enough" was never acceptable in the Malmstadt lab, and his students and colleagues knew it. Requiring such high standards occasionally caused tension, but Howard felt he could give no less. He lived by the biblical standard of Colossians 3:23–24: "Whatever you do, work at it with all your heart, as working for the Lord, not for men, since you know that you will receive an inheritance from the Lord as a reward. It is the Lord Christ you are serving."

It troubled him that some Christians did mediocre work because of a worldview that divided church and spiritual life (the sacred) from their work or artistic life (the secular). Howard believed it was no less spiritual to be a scientist or police officer or grocer dedicated to God than to be a pastor or Bible scholar. He applauded Franky Schaeffer's book *Addicted to Mediocrity,* which challenged sacred-versus-secular thinking and urged Christians to not tolerate mediocrity, particularly in the arts.

Howard was quick to affirm excellence in the work of his colleagues. One he particularly admired was U of I professor of architecture Jim Miller. The "elegance and excellence" he pursued in his own work was clearly evident in the designs of Dr. Miller, who rose to become department chair at U of I and an internationally acclaimed designer of university campuses.

The two became fast friends. Jim Miller saw in Howard a humility that might seem contradictory in someone so driven to achieve excellence. "My first impressions of Howard were of a gentle, very talented, but down-to-earth, caring Christian brother. From that time on, he had a way of making me feel important as a professional. During the following years we developed a close bond, which I often said was deeper than that between me and my own two brothers."

When this friendship began, Dr. Miller could not have known how often his work would intertwine with Howard's over the coming years. Their collaboration would continue for thirty years, taking them to many nations and putting them together on projects that neither could have imagined beforehand. In the principles they taught, the plans they helped others to design, and the University of the Nations campuses they built, their examples of elegance and excellence live on.

6.

A Courageous Transition

Take the first step in faith. You don't have to see the whole staircase, just take the first step.
— MARTIN LUTHER KING JR.

*H*oward was sitting on a folding chair in a room of a long-abandoned hotel in Hawaii. The man sitting across from him—normally strong and confident—was visibly on edge. Finally he blurted out the reason he had invited Howard to visit; it was huge, a vision of global proportions. Calmly, Howard explained that he had heard it before and asked if he could take part in it.

It took a few moments for the other man to recover from his shock.

By the early 1970s Howard Malmstadt's scientific career was speeding like a brilliant comet. His research and publications about spectroscopy, chemistry, and electronic instrumentation attracted international attention and respect. He was teaching the "short course" worldwide, and more invitations were pouring in. He was mentoring PhD students who were going on to establish reputations of their own. And his peers in academic, scientific, and government circles were lavishing awards, grants, and speaking invitations on him.

He was the last person anyone expected to make a major mid-career change.

Even as his career was soaring, Howard never strayed from the spiritual life he learned as a child in the Marinette Presbyterian Church. He did not talk about a "salvation experience" in the sense of a specific, dramatic moment of conversion to faith in Jesus Christ. It may be that there was such a moment in his life, but his normal reticence on personal matters may have kept him from sharing it openly. In any case, he viewed himself as a committed Christian throughout his life.

During his college years, Howard sought out Christian fellowship groups. And when he and Carolyn married, they faithfully attended the local Presbyterian church with their children, viewing the congregation as their extended family. Howard was no ordinary pew sitter; he believed in getting involved fully. He taught Sunday school at several levels and served on various church boards over the years. Prior to accepting the instructor position at U of I in 1951, he and Carolyn had talked with Presbyterian Mission Board members about the possibility of taking a foreign mission assignment.

The Malmstadts decided not to go that direction at the time, but Howard did not view his academic work as a holding pattern until he could "really" serve the Lord in missions. Presbyterian Reformed theology emphasizes serving God with excellence in one's vocation or calling, and Howard pursued his chemistry career as a way of blessing humanity and being a positive influence for God. Barbara Opperman, wife of one of his fellow professors, spoke of Howard's active faith while he was at U of I: "Howard never hesitated to share his faith with his graduate students. And when he was presenting papers at scientific meetings, he acknowledged the Creator."[1]

Then, in the late 1960s, Howard heard a talk by David Wilkerson, author of *The Cross and the Switchblade.* Wilkerson's story sparked Howard's interest in the charismatic movement and the gifts of the Holy Spirit. Howard investigated these phenomena by reading books by Dr. Francis Schaeffer, Episcopal priest Dennis Bennett, and others. The more he read, the more he pursued a deeper intimacy with God. And rather than discard all he had experienced to that point, he integrated his pursuit of excellence in the context of being led by the Holy Spirit.

One evidence of this is in his book *Courageous Leaders Transforming Their World,* in which he tells how to form a "Council" that sets objectives through corporate prayer: "This is a committed leadership team of members of one's community or organization who begin by seeking God and allowing Him to birth a vision to be transformational servants....An awareness of God's character and insight into what would bring joy to His heart would open the door to creative ideas that might be translated into an Overall Objective."[2] Howard's passions for teamwork and creative collaboration were set firmly in the context of seeking God's wisdom, in effect merging the strengths of the Reformed and charismatic streams of faith.

Another influence on Howard's life came about more indirectly. In the early 1970s, his daughter Cynthia had become involved with Youth With A Mission (YWAM), and in his own professional travels, Howard made a point of visiting several of YWAM's ministry centers around the world to learn more about the activities of the multidenominational mission group. He became deeply impressed with the young Christians he met, who were passionately intent on fulfilling the Great Commission[3] in a variety of ways. As he saw people from a wide variety of backgrounds contributing their unique gifts and talents to the group, his eyes were opened to the possibilities of applying his own scientific and educational knowledge to the task of reaching out to people in need all over the world.

In particular, he began to see a bigger picture of what it could mean to become a missionary while continuing to pursue his loves of teaching and analytical chemistry.

Meanwhile, Howard's U of I lab was increasingly active in pursuing research grants from government agencies. Colleagues report he was highly successful, but this process of application and reapplication became an annual treadmill, demanding increasing time and energy that pulled him away from the research work and mentoring he so enjoyed. Furthermore, Howard's reputation for

attracting top students, funding, and recognition stirred some jeal-
ousy in the highly competitive and status-sensitive academic and
scientific world. Amid the politics and pressures of this environment, the stage was quietly being set for a major change in his life.

Meanwhile, YWAM founder Loren Cunningham was leading
his young mission group into a new level of training. In February
1975, YWAM leaders gathered in Hilo, Hawaii, and decided to
devote three days to prayer and fasting to seek God's guidance. As
they prayed, the phrase "modular education" kept popping into
their minds. Loren, who has a master's degree in administration
supervision in education from the University of Southern California, and another participant who was a college dean, agreed that
this was not a known educational term. Nevertheless, the group
was unanimous in their belief that this was what God was saying.
They didn't really discuss or pray about the "university" idea at
that point. They believed the modular education concept—still
mostly undefined—would be applied from preschool to "tertiary
education."

Loren left Hilo to take part in a spiritual leadership conference in the Midwest where he spoke on hearing God's voice. As an
illustration, he spoke of the prayer meeting in Hilo and mentioned
the phrase "modular education" they had heard. Little did Loren
know who was in the audience listening to his message.

The early 1970s brought a convergence of events and relationships that would profoundly affect the Malmstadt family and
its relationship with YWAM. One such event was an InterVarsity
Christian Fellowship meeting at U of I, where Howard and Carolyn were invited to tell their life story. One of the students present was Tom Bloomer, who was struck by a comment Carolyn
made during her talk: "I have two daughters, and I'd sure like
them to meet some young people like you." Seeing how bright
and attractive Carolyn was, Tom thought, "I'd like to meet your
daughters!" He did meet one two months later when Howard
brought Cynthia to a prayer meeting. Afterward she walked up to
Tom and introduced herself. As Tom would comment later about
her initiative, "She was her father's daughter!"

Their relationship began to blossom during Tom's senior year. But as he neared graduation in the spring of 1972, Tom felt God leading him to join YWAM and go to Germany to help a young YWAM leader named David Boyd, who was organizing outreaches to military bases. This would mean a year away from Cynthia, so Tom invited her to Germany for Christmas at his brother's home. It was there Tom asked her to marry him. This engagement wasn't fully embraced by the Malmstadts at the time. Howard was in favor, but Carolyn was less certain. Tom, after all, was a longhaired hippie wanting Cynthia to join him in working unsalaried in overseas missions with YWAM. However, on the morning of their August 1973 wedding in Urbana, Illinois, Carolyn prayed and received a confirmation. And at the ceremony, Howard prayed a beautiful blessing over the new couple, and by the end of it, there was not a dry eye in the place.

The newlyweds stayed on that autumn to complete Cynthia's teaching commitment in the Midwest. But four months later, she and Tom returned to Europe, first taking a School of Evangelism (SOE), then joining YWAM in French Ministries. Later, in Switzerland, they found themselves talking with Loren about an upcoming spiritual-leadership conference in St. Louis at which Loren, Joy Dawson, and Campbell McAlpine would be speaking. Howard had asked them to pass on whatever they were learning about leadership principles, so they mailed the conference brochure to him. They even prayed that he would attend the conference—no simple matter given all his responsibilities at U of I. Nevertheless, he was able to attend and sat attentively as Loren spoke.

As Loren relates it, "After the talk, this man came up and introduced himself as Howard Malmstadt. He said, 'I'm so glad you brought up modular education. You know, the Lord showed me the same thing...and I've written some textbooks about it!'" Howard was catching a glimpse of how his educational training could be helpful in developing spiritual leaders.

For Loren, this was the first time an educator confirmed this modular concept. More important, in Howard he observed a man who was "humble, straightforward, gentle as a lamb, yet not weak." He invited Howard to work with him on a curriculum-development project and to colead educational seminars. As they began strategizing together, Loren was amazed by their common vision. "I felt so 'one' with him." The budding friendship of these two visionaries would prove deeply rewarding to both.

One of the stories Loren shared with his new friend was about an all-night prayer meeting in November 1973 in Kaneohe, Hawaii, during which Loren and three other staff heard God speak the word *Kona.* Loren told Howard that they knew little about the place, only that it was a small fishing village on the Big Island of Hawaii. The location was not obviously strategic, yet in that same prayer time, Loren had seen a vision of a lighthouse shining toward Asia.

The next morning, the staff did not immediately share with students what they had heard during the night; instead, they had challenged them to wait on the Lord and see if He said the same things to them. One by one, as they waited on the Lord, their impressions were shared. The first student said she saw a large letter *K.* Another student had the word *Kona* (not knowing what that meant). Others mentioned a farm, a ship in a harbor . . . and a white house on a hill. Based on this guidance, Loren sent a scouting team to Kona, and within a few months YWAMers began moving to the Big Island, occupying whatever rented facilities they could find (including a farm). Loren told Howard he was sure Kona would play a key role in YWAM's future, but he didn't yet know how.

By 1977 Kona's key role was becoming clear through a series of amazing events. YWAM had just bought its first Kona property—the old Greenwell farmhouse known as King's Mansion. This white house on a hill was exactly as envisioned in the Kaneohe prayer meeting! YWAM leaders also had placed a bid on Kona's bankrupt Pacific Empress Hotel and sensed that God was going to give them that forty-five-acre property. At a leadership meeting that spring they also heard God speak about developing a missions-oriented "university of the Spirit."

One of Loren's guiding principles is that God speaks today—just as He did in Bible times—to those who listen for His voice and are willing to obey. But when God began speaking to him and the other leaders about a university, Loren grew concerned about the implications of the word. "I did not want to 'do university.' I felt the name would raise too many expectations." Loren asked God if they could call it something else. He sensed God's answer: that the Lord wanted to redeem the very name *university* through what He would do in YWAM.

In August 1977 Loren flew to Finland to meet with YWAM's International Council. He took that opportunity to share with the council the vision of a university. Again, the leaders went to prayer for direction. Afterward, Loren polled them, and each one had words of confirmation. Last to speak was Jim Dawson, who shared Scripture passages related to training, then said, "I believe this is what God is saying we are to do." Just then, the phone rang with a call from Hawaii informing Loren that an earlier deal for the Pacific Empress Hotel had fallen through and that it was available to YWAM to buy. Down from its asking price of $8 million, YWAM could have it for $1.8 million with a $30,000 down payment. Over the next few days, Loren scrambled to raise the down payment, and by September the first group of YWAMers were moving in.

To a casual observer, the old hotel was no prize. The grounds were overgrown with weeds and vines; the buildings were dilapidated and occupied by rats, roaches, and squatters; and the electrical and plumbing systems were in a sorry state. As the zealous young missionaries pitched in to clear the land, the acronym YWAM took on a new meaning: "Youth With A Machete." It would take months of hard labor to restore the property, but these YWAMers were up to the task, for they now had the beginnings of their first campus.

There was one more major aspect to the confirmation about YWAM's having a university. From the Finland meeting, Loren and his wife Darlene, and Jim and Joy Dawson had flown directly to Dallas to meet with Leonard Ravenhill, a well-known author and prophetic teacher, for a prearranged time of prayer. A couple of hours into the prayer time, Leonard spoke out, "God, You're speaking to me about a spiritual university…in Kona. I pray that You will bring this forth!"

Loren sat there silently, wondering what to say. At that point, only the International Leadership Team knew about the vision to start a university.

Leonard prayed the same prayer two more times, and after the second time, Loren couldn't hold it in any longer. He told Leonard that YWAM's leaders had just received guidance to do that very thing. Characteristically, Leonard was unruffled, saying, "That's the right thing to do; that's what the Lord is saying."

The next confirmation came shortly after Loren and Darlene moved into Building 3 of the old hotel in the fall of 1977. Howard flew to Kona to pay them a visit. By this time, Loren had learned of Howard's accomplishments in academia. He wanted to offer his distinguished guest proper hospitality, but the only furnishings he and Darlene had were two metal folding chairs. Seated in this humble setting, Loren broke the news to Howard about YWAM's plan to build a university. It was a story Howard loved to tell in the years to come.

"It was the only time I've seen Loren nervous. He told me God had said [YWAM] was to have a university. Loren was so shocked when I said, 'Oh, God already told me that!' "[4]

Loren pressed for more details. At that point, only a few YWAM leaders had been told of the university vision, so he wondered if the news had leaked. Howard assured Loren he had heard from God, just as they had. He explained that he had been approached about three different university presidency positions, which would advance his career and provide financial security for his family. But as he prayed about the offers, Howard heard God say to him that he was not to accept any of them. Rather, he was to go to Hawaii. God said He was going to give YWAM a university there and He wanted Howard to be a part of it—not as president but as international provost.

"When did you hear this?" Loren wanted to know.

"Last April," Howard replied. Loren knew this was just weeks after the prayer meeting of YWAM leaders in Kona at which the vision first came. Another confirmation. Now to the stunned YWAM leader, Howard said, "So, I'm willing to be a part of this." Loren's eager response was How soon can we start?

This trip to Kona followed a difficult time of prayer and soul searching by Howard and Carolyn over the options before them. On one hand, there was all the security, creativity, and recognition of a highly successful career. On the other hand was a missions organization full of ideas and zeal but with precious few resources or facilities for launching something as ambitious as a university.

For Howard, the key to the decision was the word of the Lord. He looked beyond the comfortable circumstances of his career and listened to what he believed God was calling him to do. This decision cost Howard in many ways over the years to follow, disrupting his home and family life and taking him far from his wife and family for weeks and months at a time.

Having said yes to God, Howard started phasing out his doctoral students in an orderly manner. His concern for his students meant that he spent the next three years working with each one to complete his graduate studies under his guidance.

This transition period created unique opportunities for Howard. He described it years later at a U of N workshop in 1995 in Restenas, Sweden. The environment he was leaving was full of exciting discoveries and a stimulating creative atmosphere. Those at the university thought he had lost it. As word of his decision got out, many came to him to try to understand what was motivating such an astonishing decision. Some spent hours probing his beliefs. Howard commented, "Previously when I would bring up what I believe, I would usually get a polite but quick response that they had another appointment to meet with somebody. The Lord has mysterious ways of working in our lives."

Dr. Derek Chignell, formerly a Wheaton College professor, says people still remember a chapel talk Howard gave at that time. The message was, "It's never too late to be a missionary, even at age fifty-five!"

Chris Enke was one who admired his former professor's decision: "Howard did a courageous thing—he left his team of more than twenty doctoral students, excellent labs, research funding support, and a successful career to go work with YWAM."

The decision was all the more amazing to colleagues, considering that Howard would be unpaid while attempting to build a university "by faith" with an all-volunteer staff. Many in academic circles wondered if he would abandon his scientific roots. As the years unfolded, various factors conspired to keep Howard in touch. First, he continued to receive scientific and academic awards which translated into travel and speaking opportunities. He also attended professional conferences such as Pittcon on an annual basis. These were opportunities for him to catch up with old students and colleagues and to stay abreast of scientific advances. Also, he continued teaching the "short course" up until 2003.

Gary Hieftje, one of Howard's graduate students in the 1960s, describes Howard's devotion to his students:

> The relationship between Howard Malmstadt and his students was not a transient one, limited to the period of graduate study. Rather, that period was an introduction, to what would in most cases become a life-long friendship. Despite Howard's grueling travel schedule, he often managed to attend lectures by his former group members, and was frequently present when they received awards. Kind words of congratulations and support were all the more important from someone so respected.

As the number of Howard's graduates grew, they became an extended family, as it were. Modeling their academic "father" in approaches to research, teaching, and relationships, they were "mutually very supportive, attending each other's presentations and award ceremonies and announcing with pride that they also were former graduates (or second- or third-generation members) of the Malmstadt group. It is both interesting and amazing to examine almost any list of awards in the field of analytical chemistry and to note how many are members of this extended family."

While Howard did not disappear entirely from the analytical chemistry scene, understandably his research and publication contributions tapered off as his interests and energies began to focus in a new direction. He set his heart and mind to carry out the vision of YWAM's global university.

7.

Laying New Foundations

The loftier the building, the deeper must the foundation be laid.
— THOMAS À KEMPIS

*The Hawaii sun beat down on the volunteers working with machetes,
other tools, and bare hands to clear the hotel grounds from the effects
of years of neglect. Working alongside the others was a middle-aged man
with his trademark banana-stained overalls. While others wondered about
the point of this backbreaking work, Howard in his overalls was no doubt
dreaming of the university to be built where weeds and grasses now ruled.*

The momentous decision to join YWAM in 1977 set in
motion a wave of events for the Malmstadt family. Howard peti-
tioned for retirement from the University of Illinois. U of I asked
him to accept a ranking of professor emeritus, which he did. He
stopped accepting new doctoral candidates but felt he should
allow his current students to complete their work under his guidance rather than force them to find new sponsors. This resulted in
a three-year transition period, after which Howard and Carolyn
sold their much-loved home in Urbana and moved to Kailua-
Kona, Hawaii.

"As you can imagine it was a highly emotional time for us all
to be leaving Illinois and going into the more uncertain future,"
recalls Carolyn. "Some years later Howard told me that if he had

stayed on the regular payroll for a couple of months, his pension would have been significantly greater, but he felt that should not be a consideration. I think his heart ached when he would go back to U of I and realize what he had left behind, especially when the Kona scene was such a contrast. However he never indicated that he was sorry he had made the move. I don't think he ever thought it was a mistake. He was being obedient to his leading."

One way we can measure the feelings Howard had in leaving his U of I life is by the fact that he was never able to return to his office there to clear it of his belongings. Eventually, U of I's chemistry department boxed up everything and shipped it to his Michigan home. As Carolyn notes, "This might be a demonstration of how he was wired—concentrating on what lay ahead and leaving what was behind for those who are designed for dealing with that." Clearly, Howard continued to miss his former life, even as an exciting new chapter was unfolding.

In keeping with his temperament, the moment Howard said yes to YWAM, his heart moved to Kona. Starting in January 1978, Howard came to Kona regularly to work with Loren to form the concepts by which the university should be designed. That September, Loren led a Crossroads Discipleship Training School (CDTS), YWAM's first entry-level school for older students and a requirement for new staff. Howard and Carolyn joined that CDTS class, humbly fulfilling the expectations of any new recruit rather than demanding his credentials merit him an exception. In that class were a number of others who went on to be major leaders in YWAM.

As Loren Cunningham and Howard began to work on the framework of a university for YWAM, and more particularly a first campus in Kona, they realized they needed an architect on the team. Howard mentioned that he knew an architect who was also experienced in campus design both in the United States and overseas. Howard was thinking of his friend Jim Miller back at U of I. At that time, Jim was involved in planning university campuses in various countries in Asia and traveled often in connection with that work. Howard called Jim and asked him to stop in Kona on his way to a project in Pakistan.

That visit led to a four-day planning session in which Howard and Loren peppered Jim with questions. Jim freely gave his advice and continued on his way to Pakistan, eventually returning home to Urbana. A short while later, Howard, the master recruiter, called Jim in Urbana and invited him to help implement the campus plan he had outlined in Kona. Jim had by then become part of Howard's life in a hands-on way. He and Howard would spend intense planning weeks in Kona, then return to Urbana and carve out time to collaborate there as well.

The two needed all the vision they could muster to create a university on the Kona site. The existing hotel buildings were barely usable; the grounds were a mess; and the rocky volcanic soil would make new construction difficult. Howard's mind would sometimes go back to the fully developed campus he had left behind in Illinois. Yet, he and Jim dreamed and planned with a fury. "One of our favorite things to do after our late-night meetings was to go to Kailua Village and get macadamia-nut ice cream cones," recalls Jim. "Very refreshing, it was."

Both men were refreshed as well by the opportunity to design a university starting with a clean slate. In between Jim's visits, a three-way team was forming in Kona: Loren and Darlene Cunningham and Howard. Loren's role was to cast the vision of missions and the principles by which the emerging university would fit into that most basic part of YWAM's calling. Darlene was the implementer, serving as the first director of operations. Howard had responsibility for academics and campus development.

Loren recalls, "It was easy to serve [Howard]. We had such agreement in spirit, deferring to each other's strengths. In twenty-six years of working together, we never had an argument." Such was the trust between these men that they were able to work alongside each other without constantly looking over each other's shoulders.

By September of 1978, approximately one hundred YWAMers were living on the new Kona campus. They divided up work responsibilities, including kitchen duty, cleaning, and grounds maintenance. It was a pioneer environment, more oriented to the basics of survival than the lofty ideals of a university. Howard had to roll up his sleeves to work with the others and learn patience as he looked down the road at what could be. Indeed, he and Loren craved extended times to talk about the future.

Before the first university building was designed, a spiritual foundation needed to be laid. For Howard, the foundation lay in Matthew 28:18–20: "Then Jesus came to them and said, 'All authority in heaven and on earth has been given to me. Therefore go and make disciples of all nations, baptizing them in the name of the Father and of the Son and of the Holy Spirit, and teaching them to obey everything I have commanded you. And surely I am with you always, to the very end of the age.'"

This passage, commonly called the Great Commission, represents what Howard and other YWAM pioneers believed was the core mandate for their new university. Howard summarized this in the phrase "discipling the nations." This encompasses influencing the worldviews, policies, and institutions of a nation. As Howard often explained, all universities are discipling nations—"for better or worse"—in a variety of ways.

"Some of these ways are obvious," Howard said in a 1995 University of the Nations workshop, "in that international students make up a significant part of many student bodies. After graduation, many of these students return to their home countries and apply what they have learned.

"Some ways are less obvious, such as when a particular worldview might be presented implicitly or explicitly in the course material."

Howard believed his new university should do more than just teach courses. Based on his military and academic experiences, he believed that an effective learning environment was as important as the course work. One strong formative influence was a six-week short course Howard had taken between his junior and senior years at the University of Wisconsin. Only Howard and one other were regular students, the rest being professionals. Instead of being concerned about grades, they were eager to learn something new. The atmosphere was a mixture of friendly, relaxed relationships and intense study. Howard commented, "They wanted to help each other, share their experiences and understanding of the course content. This course opened my eyes to the great importance of the learning environment."

Howard distilled that experience into a core principle he called "live/learn," meaning that teachers and students live in community in a comprehensive learning environment. This environment allows the teacher to take an interest in the individual student, including helping each one through personal problems that otherwise would get in the way of learning. The transfer of academic "head" knowledge by itself can be sterile; in the context of a focused yet caring community, much more can be conveyed and learned. Far from its being a simple homogenous community, Howard believed the ideal learning environment should be cross-cultural, cross-generational, and familial.

A second element of Howard's foundational planning was his defining what it meant for courses to be modular. To him a course module was a single course of study taken over a twelve-week period. He foresaw YWAM offering foundation modules such as the Discipleship Training School (DTS) and various core courses. Students could build on those foundations in a number of ways, rearranging subsequent courses to suit their emerging interests.

Another principle he dubbed the "top-down approach." By this, he meant that the material should be presented first in an overview sense, then with increasing details, leading to a hands-on application of what was just learned. In the years that followed, this developed into a course structure consisting of a three-month lecture phase, followed by a two- or three-month field assignment or outreach phase, often in another country. During the field assignment, students would be faced with challenges that would motivate them to go back and take specific courses to give them the skills they lacked. The result would be students who were motivated and being equipped for real-world needs.

Referring to his own very personal experiences of God during World War II, Howard believed that the new university should allow for "revelation" to occur for the staff and students. In his words, he wanted to ensure that the "Holy Spirit is continuously welcome—not shut out because of our techniques or content." He spoke often of the university's being founded on the "Word of the Lord."

Reflecting on his own graduate-school experience, Howard saw the enormous benefit of an environment rich in resources—not just fancy equipment but access to people in a wide range of professional disciplines and "exciting and stimulating environments that draw out of students their creative giftings."

In particular, his work over the years with research students taught him the value of opportunities for one-on-one relationships. As he put it, "the one-on-one for ten to thirty minutes can often be more significant than several hours of lectures." Relationships were always a major part of Howard's thinking and practice.

Howard had written over a dozen textbooks during his U of I years to pass on the principles and lab techniques he was learning. In the new university, at first called Pacific & Asia Christian University (PACU)—later changed to the University of the Nations (U of N)—he challenged those working with him to create educational resources that could "spread worldwide and literally impact every area of society." He was no longer content to have influence only within the field of analytical chemistry; in fact, his former role was starting to seem narrow in the light of the expanded vision he was now exploring.

Those early days in Kona were characterized by a pioneering spirit. Of course, there was much work to do in clearing the land, chasing out the rats, and repairing the broken-down buildings. Howard's son Jon fixed up an office in the room under their home for him to use, and Howard turned down offers of other office space until the Impact Center was built. The campus had no air conditioning, and the furnishings were downright Spartan compared to his U of I facilities, but despite the relatively uncomfortable setting, there was a growing sense of excitement about what the future held. The PACU leadership spent countless hours in prayer meetings to seek what God was saying to the young mission about the university. Everyone shared an expectancy that God would give them general principles and specific strategies to use in accomplishing their goals.

One of Howard's ideas was to form nonprofit institutes to research and prototype discoveries and act as liaison between PACU and for-profit companies that could turn the discoveries into commercial products. The institutes, staffed by paid and volunteer workers, would buffer PACU from financial entanglements that could jeopardize PACU's nonprofit and all-volunteer status. Howard had designed an automated clinical analysis instrument back at U of I and now approached a corporation to partner with his prototype shop located in the industrial area in Kona. He also proposed that they provide additional money to fund the first structure for PACU which became known as the Administration Building. This building was the early home of a team of architects, design engineers, and others trained in construction that Howard started to assemble. Among these people was Mike Franke, a designer who with his wife, Barbara, followed the Malmstadts into YWAM from Urbana. Mike found himself working for Hal Davis, the resident architect from Alabama, and a diverse group that included a young civil engineer named David Ross and electrical engineer Bill Goulding. In all, seven people and their desks were crammed into a fourteen-by-twenty-two-foot office.

In addition to the pressures of space, the agenda was ambitious—designing half a dozen buildings at once. Also, from their past experience the team members were used to having their own way on construction projects, having developed confidence and aggressive techniques in the working world. Egos jostled for influence and greater responsibility. Howard, characteristically, stayed committed to the need for consensus, letting each person contribute his own views.

The diverse nature of the team led to some funny moments. On one occasion, Brian Pollard, a talented but serious illustrator from England, was hard at work when unabashed jokester John Carson, a construction guy from Virginia, leaned over Brian's work, exclaimed "That's horrible," and walked off. According to Mike, Brian's face turned white, and his eyes got "as big as fried eggs." It took some time for Brian to appreciate Mike's explanation that this was John's way of being friendly.

On another occasion, Hal was explaining something to the group in his slow, methodical way, and David kept jumping in to finish his sentences. Finally, Hal stopped and patiently commented that while he was open to constructive criticism, he would like to finish his own sentences. David piped up, "Well, you talk too slow, I talk too much...we all have our growth areas!"

Humor was needed as the team grappled with seemingly insurmountable challenges. Their idea of having international field assignments follow their course modules was expensive and logistically difficult. Also, the goal of accreditation implied the need for lots of lab space and equipment, not to mention salaries for the faculty and an administrative structure for the university.

One day in a team meeting, the challenge became overwhelming, and the team complained to Howard that they simply didn't have the resources to accomplish the task. Howard responded with a story from his war years. "I remember one time things had gotten pretty bad on the ship," he related. "I decided to go to the commanding officer (CO) with one of those 'with all due respect' speeches, explaining all the reasons why we couldn't get the job done." Howard's CO had glared back and made it very clear that the work would need to be done anyway. As Howard struggled to paraphrase the coarse words used by his CO, one of the team offered helpfully, "in no uncertain terms?" and Howard gratefully used that euphemism to stand for the original message. Although Howard softened the impact, the meaning was unchanged: lack of resources was no excuse.

This was one of many times in which Howard would identify with the struggles of the team, drawing on his own failures and shortcomings. Then he would inspire others to learn from his own mistakes, express his confidence in them, and hold them accountable for results.

With the foundational principles in place for the university as a whole, Howard, Loren, and Jim were ready in 1981 to prepare what became the Campus Development Guide.[1] As the preface to the 1986 update states, "While the bricks and mortar of a university building are definitely less important than the people and the program, once established, they set the permanent continuing environment in which the university will either thrive or languish."

The guide continues with policies about the expected student population of PACU. These policies included the expected mix of single, divorced, married with or without children, retired, male/female ratios ("a numerical balance"), undergraduate/postgraduate mixes, faculty/student ratios (ranging from 1:250 for lectures to 1:12 for graduate lab courses) and even the evolving mix of Western/Asia-Pacific nationalities, with the latter becoming "at least 50 percent over time" (note: the university continues to maintain a fifty percent ratio of international students).[2]

As the guide further states, "PACU is unique in that none of the staff is salaried. Staff even contribute most of the cost of their room and board." This policy was—and is today for the U of N—a two-edged sword. While the operating expenses of the university would be greatly reduced, staff people would need to rely on support from families, friends, home churches, or other resources. Over the years, this challenge has given rise to many stories of God's faithfulness as individuals and families have struggled to be obedient. Visiting faculty would be generally given travel expenses and honoraria, and other programs would develop over the years to enable people to volunteer their time and skills on a short-term basis in exchange for room and board. However, to this day this no-salary policy stands as a hallmark characteristic of YWAM and its university.

Loren had received a "word of the Lord" in 1975 about the seven spheres of influence in society (sometimes called "mind molders"), and these were used as general guidelines in developing PACU's colleges and corresponding building clusters. For *Family,* there was a College of Counseling and Health Care; for *Religion,* College of Christian Ministries. The College of *Education* is self-explanatory, while the College of Performing Arts addressed the arena of *Entertainment and Sports.* The College of Communication would focus on the areas of *Media and Public Communication.* The new College of Science and Technology—which Howard served as its first dean—would teach the broad spectrum of *Science and Economics.* Finally, a College of Humanities and International Studies was formed, corresponding to the sphere of *Government and Public Leadership.*

The Development Guide continued by evaluating the needs of the many academic, support, and "village"-oriented activities planned for the campus, down to square footage required, number of hours spent on various activities, and even considering the optimal orientation of the buildings, including such factors as sun, ocean views, and upslope (*mauka* in Hawaiian) day breezes versus down slope (*makai*) night breezes. One of the planned buildings was particularly significant in showing forethought not only for the ongoing development of the Kona campus but also for the outward focus of the U of N. This building was (and is) called the IMPACT Design Center. "IMPACT is an acronym for International Missions Programs for the Assembling of Consulting and Technical teams. These teams provide opportunities for Christians with technical skills to be witnesses on the mission field while using their professional expertise."

The Counseling and Health Care Center, also at the gateway to the Kona campus, was designed with a similar outward focus in mind, providing a range of counseling services—psychological, family, financial, and legal—to the local community both as a means of training and as a service to the people of Kona.

The campus to be built in Kona to facilitate this new university had in its very DNA the intent to be a blessing to the local community and to the nations.

Howard's family also contributed to the birthing and nurturing of the university. Carolyn helped start the campus library, and son Jon helped Howard by finishing the half-basement rooms in a home built by the Sundseth Construction Company for their family just off campus. The new home quickly became a haven for staff members from the intense work environment and sparse surroundings of the campus.

Weekly planning meetings were held in the Malmstadt home. Howard and Carolyn also hosted many staff members for "family time" and home-cooked meals. Donna Livingston, a YWAMer from Urbana, remembers going there for dinner. "Carolyn served us a roast and real potatoes....It was heavenly being able to sit on a couch or play with the Franke [Mike and Barbara] kids on a clean floor."

In this tangible way, Howard and Carolyn did what they could to reduce the stresses of campus living for the team. They were modeling the principle of focusing not on what they didn't have but rather on what was "in their hands."

Jon contributed to the campus in other ways, including building play equipment for the toddler area that became known as Keiki Corner. When Carolyn's health required her to return to their Michigan home in 1987, Jon divided his time between Michigan and Kona for that winter and the next, finally moving to Michigan in 1989 after the Kona house was sold. In Michigan, Jon cared for his mother and dealt with emails, financial matters, and all the burdens of home ownership for the frequent times his father was away. Howard often commented how his own ministry through the following years would not have been possible without Carolyn's ongoing prayers and Jon's faithful service. However necessary Carolyn's move had been, it meant long stretches of time apart, an ongoing burden for all of them.

Over the years, other family members were involved in different ways in Howard's ministry. Tom and Cynthia Bloomer continued serving in YWAM, enjoying the enriching experience of working alongside Howard in building the U of N. Alice and her husband, Phil Magner, provided encouragement and the joy of their sons, Jonathan and Paul. These last two and Philip Bloomer, when he came along, spent many happy, active hours as babies and toddlers playing with Grandpa Howard, who took great delight in his little grandsons.

Initially, the name Pacific & Asia Christian University was chosen for the new university because of its Hawaii location. But as other expressions of YWAM's university were developing on six continents, it became obvious that the name PACU would not cover the worldwide scope and unity of YWAM's higher education goals. Therefore, the Board of Regents unanimously adopted the new name, University of the Nations, at their meeting in 1988. The name change took place officially on June 2, 1989.[3]

University of the Nations quickly became shortened to U of N. At times, that abbreviation has been confused with the UN (United Nations), leading to some apocryphal stories linking Howard to that better-known organization.

Howard constantly pushed everyone in the U of N to strive for excellence. At a chapel service he talked about the "ideal" Christian university. Some of his comments from the service follow, giving a glimpse of the inspired vision that he was constantly putting in front of his listeners:

"I am often asked, 'How is a Christian university different from other universities?' First and foremost, I believe a Christian university is a people—a people called by God, a people of eternal destiny."

At the service, Howard described an environment of people from many backgrounds, functions, and responsibilities. He said that the shared focus is on the "Creator of the universe. The buildings and the equipment are important," he said, "but people are the life of a university."

He talked about his U of I doctoral students whom he had challenged to consider the "truly ideal solution" for their research projects and how he also challenged himself to think about the characteristics of an ideal Christian university. Here are some of the characteristics Howard presented:

1. The people, who are the university, would know God intimately, and their hearts would be on fire to make Him known.

2. The people would be committed and become engaged in the Great Commission given by Jesus in Matthew 28:18–20.

3. The campus community would express the love of Jesus in numerous tangible ways.

4. The people would work together in unity and would be a catalyst for unity in the body of Christ (John 17:20–23).

5. The people would be obedient to the Word of God.

6. The programs, courses, and activities would be inspired by the Holy Spirit and be designed to release God's gifts of creativity in students and staff and the people groups they serve in ministries.

Howard also invited his audience to consider other characteristics they would add to this list. He asked, "Is it possible to reach
the ideal? Yes, I believe that it is, if we seek diligently to remain
open to impartation from our Creator."

Howard affirmed that developing Christian universities for
God's purposes and by His Word is a valid calling. This requires
men and women who seek God in prayer, counting the cost in
order to affect the future. This process will include times when
God "confirms their thoughts," and other times when God "shows
them a better way." The programs and ministries that result
should "all contribute to building a people—a people called and
taught of God, a people of destiny, a people who will fully play
their part in bringing a great multitude [of nations] before God's
throne." (See Revelation 7:9–10.)

Howard concluded this memorable chapel service with a broad
prophetic challenge: "Until that day, He seeks for men, for
women, to follow His plans, including His plans for developing
the University of the Nations and other Christian universities—
true universities committed to His vision, His ways of teaching,
of managing, of communicating, His ways of working together
in community—in unity....He is with us, and He will guide us
toward the ideal."

Howard would be the first to admit that the U of N hadn't—
and hasn't yet—reached the ideal. But he would be the last to stop
the pursuit of that ideal. Once, Howard was asked what kind of
leadership was needed to take the U of N into the future. He
answered in part: "The potential for this university is so fantastic
it is impossible. And that is good if we can have leaders who really
understand that. If we do the possible and let God do the impossible, this university will be fantastic."[4]

8.

A Passion for People

Never seem more learned than the people you are with. Wear your learning like a pocket watch and keep it hidden. Do not pull it out to count the hours, but give the time when you are asked.

—LORD CHESTERFIELD

*H*oward was at a scientific conference in Pittsburgh, standing on an island in the middle of the street. Alex Scheeline, a colleague from U of I, was on the other side of multiple lanes of traffic. At a break in the traffic, they both headed out at a brisk walk to get to the other, and they met in the middle. Howard immediately started talking, asking how Alex was, asking about the family, asking about the lab. In the blink of an eye, the traffic reappeared amd surged around them. Alex paints the picture: "So there we are, within inches of being flattened onto the pavement, and he's looking straight at me, oblivious to the cars, oblivious to the entire universe except what I'm telling him. But of course he had a meeting to get to (when didn't he?), so after absorbing a year's worth of information in a few seconds, he turned, finished crossing the street, and disappeared into an adjacent hotel. Except he didn't bother to notice the traffic. There were screeching tires and shaken drivers (and I was still in the middle of the street), but he was focused on getting to his meeting, so he again didn't see the cars. He made each person he talked to think he or she was the only person he knew—in that brief window between such encounters with untold thousands of other people."

Howard's personality was such that almost everyone who met him briefly or knew him for many years used the same word to describe him: warmth. He was a rare breed: a brilliant scientist, filled with passion for the forward progress of analytical chemistry and spectroscopy; and yet he was a flesh-and-blood person, even more interested in the individual scientists than in the science. In the creation of this book, dozens of his former students and faculty colleagues were interviewed, and consistently they remarked about how Howard Malmstadt valued them, listened to them, and energized them in pursuit of their goals.

Howard's enthusiasm was contagious. Many have remarked that they found themselves accomplishing far more under Howard's encouragement than they would have on their own. One such student was Bonner Denton, who received his PhD under Howard in 1972. Dr. Denton went on to become a much-honored professor of chemistry and geosciences at the University of Arizona, publishing more than 150 articles on his advances in spectroscopy and chemistry. "I have a deep appreciation for Howard's personal guidance. He was a man of true wisdom and genius, with a unique perspective on science and humankind," Bonner comments.

Chris Enke, who went on to become a chemistry professor at Princeton University, Michigan State, and finally the University of New Mexico, describes their mentoring relationship as follows: "Howard inspired tremendous loyalty in his students by the way he treated them. Even though I was a student, he always treated me as a colleague. And he shared royalties with me fully right from the start." When some colleagues tell Chris that he gives his own students too much credit, he passes on the attitude Howard modeled for him—there's enough credit to go around.

Howard also had a major role in Chris Enke's spiritual journey. "Howard made me hungry by what he was and what he shared about his faith," he recalled. Years later Chris spoke of Howard as the "father I needed, the brother I never had...a mentor, colleague, and friend." Clearly, their relationship went far beyond a cordial working partnership.

Howard has been described by friends as an "extreme extrovert," but when conversing with people, he never drew attention to himself. His energy was always focused on the other persons, no matter who they were or what their positions in life. Mary Sue Ross first met Howard in the late 1970s when she came to Kona as one of the young YWAM staffers. A year later, they met again. "I was so surprised that he remembered my name," she said. "He showed genuine interest in me as a person."

Many students and staff in Kona first met Howard at the outdoor gazebo tables where YWAMers usually ate their meals. "Hi, I'm Howard," was his typical greeting. He would then probe for his new acquaintance's name, his or her involvement on campus and dreams for the future. When a student managed to redirect the conversation back to Howard, he would usually say he was involved with planning for the campus. "Most of these people had no idea that they were dining with one of the world's preeminent scientists," Forest Mims, a long-time friend and associate, says. "He never drew attention to himself."

He made friends with young and old. One time in Urbana, his former pastor Dick Foth was in town for a visit being hosted by Mike Franke. Dick was pumping Howard for his latest thoughts; like many others, he had learned to ask the question "What are you seeing?" and to expect a rich stream of insights. Dick loved the fact that Howard was always willing to translate scientific knowledge into lay terms. As they talked, Mike's two-year-old daughter Jessie came up and tugged on Howard's pant leg. "C'mon, Grandpa, let's play Buttons!" Howard turned to Dick and said simply, "I have to play Buttons," and promptly got down on the floor with Jessie to sort buttons by color and size.

YWAM pioneer Yolanda Olson remembers fondly how Howard came to each of her children's birthdays even after her husband passed away, playing games with them and truly caring for the orphans and widows. "He was constantly interested in young people of all ages, asking them about their hopes, dreams, and struggles," she recalls. Her daughter Roxanne once commented, "I could talk to him about *anything!*"

While Howard loved conversation, he was careful to avoid certain kinds of talk. If someone brought up a rumor, he would gently and quickly change the subject. If someone was despairing of the current circumstances, he would quietly remind them that "God is in control."

Howard had his share of frustrations trying to build the university with an all-volunteer staff and resources that had to be accessed "by faith." He undoubtedly reflected from time to time on the generous funding, along with buildings and well-equipped laboratories, he had left behind at U of I. How could he be expected now to accomplish anything like the achievements that had come from that environment?

Betty Barnett, who served for ten years as registrar under Howard, remembers a breakfast discussion in which she expressed disappointment at not getting the support she needed as a single woman, running the U of N catalog project single-handedly at the time. Howard responded by agreeing that the job of leaders is to provide the resources their people need. Betty pressed him to clarify that statement, as it didn't line up with her experience of his leadership for her role. "You know," he explained, "the leader should provide the desk, the chairs, the computers..."

Yet, when Betty's own father became ill, Howard didn't hesitate to release her to go for what became more than a half-year leave to care for him. His own leadership could be shortsighted in not recognizing the day-to-day needs of those under him, but he did respond to major crises in their lives.

For some, the major crisis took them away from working with Howard, and he was typically gracious in letting them go. The time came for David Ross to approach Howard and share his own dreams, which were leading him away from the U of N and all they had worked on together to concentrate more on being with his family.

For David, the hardest part was disappointing Howard. Like many others before him, he had tried many times to please Howard. The two men prayed together, and Howard released David to the new chapter in his life. Once again, Howard relinquished a piece of his own vision to let the other person pursue what was on his heart.

In Howard's own life, he released his claim on living full-time with his family. After Carolyn returned to their home in Michigan because of declining health, he continued to spend time in Kona and around the world, while always returning home to spend precious time with her.

As a result of Carolyn and Jon's move to Michigan, the Kona house was sold. When the first phase of the "Village 2" housing project was complete, the university gave Howard an apartment there to use on his many Kona visits between seasons in Michigan and traveling around the world.

Those who visited Howard in his Michigan home were treated to more of the Malmstadt hospitality. Carolyn's pies and ice cream were in abundance, and while Howard somehow managed to keep up with office work, he would take time to mingle with the family and visitors. Small wonder that family and friends referred to the place as "Camelot."

Howard had occasion to meet with royalty during his many travels on behalf of the university. "My favorite scene with Howard was when we met the king of Tonga in his royal tent on the main island of Tonga," Jim Miller recalls. He and Howard were trying to convince the king to grant them fifty acres of land to build the university campus he had requested of Loren. The king, who weighed over three hundred pounds, sat on his throne as Howard described the purpose and nature of the University of the Nations. When it was Jim's turn, he knelt down to spread out a map and show him the desired site. Jim relates, "At that point his majesty reached for his two hearing aids and inserted them, which meant he had not heard a word of what Howard had expounded. We all had a good laugh afterward."

One of Howard's favorite traditions in the early years in Kona was to go to the Old Airport Beach in Kona with family and friends for a picnic lunch. He would often clear rocks from the tidal pools to give the kids a safe place to sit and explore the various creatures. Others in his circle would follow his example, and over time others on the beach would pick up on the idea.

Howard was just as comfortable dining with kids at a beach as he was with scientists at a fine restaurant or at the table of a king. His tastes in food were as eclectic as his interests. He loved filet mignon, but he also had a great fondness for McDonald's fish sandwiches. His epiphany in this area came from his friend Graham Kerr, who was cooking for the staff at the Kona campus and had transformed himself from a gourmet chef into one preaching the virtues of healthy foods low in fat and simple carbohydrates, high in vegetables and complex carbohydrates. Howard dutifully and willingly adjusted his personal habits to favor fish and vegetables. Carolyn held him to a strict dietary regimen—as long as he was in her presence. His behavior on the road was another matter, as he always drank Coke and had a terrific fondness for desserts.

One passion remained unchanged throughout his life: he always enjoyed taking friends out for ice cream. As a scientist who could have waxed eloquent about the harmful effects of such indulgences as rich ice cream, Howard knew enough to enjoy life.

Stan Crouch's wife, Nicky, recalls their going with Howard to a Ben & Jerry's store. As the group walked along the street with their selections, Nicky's ice-cream cone fell onto the sidewalk. Howard's immediate response was to give her his own cone—for Howard, a major sacrifice, given his lifelong love of ice cream—and stoop to clean up hers. Years later, this incident still speaks to her of Howard's self-effacing character.

Howard's generosity was legendary among those who knew him best, although he was characteristically quiet about it. He donated much of the proceeds of the sale of his Kona home to the U of N for the Village 2 construction project. When in the position of a landlord, he forgave rent to Scott and Sandi Tompkins, who were just coming on staff as missionaries without sufficient financial support in place yet. For others, he quietly paid seminar fees as a means of enabling them to grow in knowledge and skills. He and Carolyn gave countless small gifts of clothing, food, tools, and so forth to many over the years. After Carolyn moved back to Michigan, Howard never hesitated to share his campus room and his beloved old Ford with others when he was off-island.

The Triplett family has a special memory in which Howard's generosity played a major part. They and others needed travel funds to return home from a conference in Budapest. The rest of the group prayed and took up a collection, and the Tripletts were given enough for their whole family to fly home. "We found out later that Howard had been a key contributor to our need," David Triplett recalls. "He was always giving of himself to others in many ways."

Derek Chignell, his long-time friend who left the chemistry department at Wheaton College to join Howard in YWAM, eulogized Howard's influence on his life at his memorial service in 2003: "For all the brilliance in chemistry, his insights into planning, his experience in academics and business, his grasp of the laws of science in the world—it is his heart that I love the most: his love for students, his joy in worship and of his devotional life." Derek went on to describe a time on the Kona campus when "Howard—completely out of the blue—turned to me, gave me a warm, warm hug, looked me directly in the eye, and said, 'Derek, I love you. You are a true, true, friend!' I will cherish that for the rest of my life."

All those who were privileged to know Howard have moments like these to cherish—and emulate—for the rest of their lives.

9.

Innovations for Missions

Real generosity towards the future lies in giving all to the present.
— ALBERT CAMUS

Douglas Feaver, who was recruited by Howard from academia to found the College of Humanities and International Studies at the U of N, recalls a conversation shortly after joining the U of N. Douglas, used to the typical campus hierarchy, asked Howard point-blank what he should be doing, and Howard's response was "If you don't know, I certainly can't help you!"

As usual, Howard instinctively put the other person's expertise and potential above his own. In the process, he built an environment in which each person could be creative to the best of his or her abilities while being free to make mistakes, thus resulting in much innovation.

In the mid-1980s, when YWAM's vision for higher education began expanding from a single campus called Pacific & Asia Christian University to a global network of campuses (later incorporated as University of the Nations), Howard Malmstadt used his office as international provost to find ways to help emerging leaders successfully plant U of N campuses around the world. Toward this end, he helped launch several innovations that greatly advanced the development of the U of N.

THE PROJECT-DEVELOPMENT LEADERSHIP SCHOOL

Fresh from their successful collaboration on the Kona campus, Howard naturally turned to Jim Miller to help in the global development process. From their discussions emerged the Project Development Leadership School (PDLS), which Howard personally led for fourteen years, beginning in 1986. Jim tells how the school became an incubator for campus development in this 2005 email:

> The PDLS was Howard's idea. I believe the idea stemmed from several factors. First, when it was decided to change from a single university in Kona (PACU) to the worldwide University of the Nations, there were a number of groups around the world that had the vision of starting branches of the University. Howard recognized that they did not have a clue about how to begin or how to carry out a wise development process. He also recognized that other YWAM projects of different types could benefit from a specialized school focusing upon principles of project-development leadership, thus the name.

In his travels, Howard recruited teams to come to the PDLS in Kona. As a result, it was common for the teaching to include simultaneous translation into one or more languages.

The focus of the PDLS course was to equip the teams to succeed in their own projects. Case studies included other projects Jim had worked on around the world. The course's emphasis on teamwork was even included in the teaching methods. Each project team would present to the class. Next, as Jim explains, the whole class "would do a charrette, or concentrated effort toward solutions to the challenge of the project."

The effects of PDLS were far-reaching, involving U of N campus master plans in Australia, Belize, Chile, Togo, Tonga, Kenya, Korea, and Twin Oaks in Texas. "It has been a joy to provide advice to the leaders of these projects and others through the years," Jim says.

The teaching style of the PDLS was highly interactive, with limited teaching from the front. As one student commented later: "I kept waiting for the course to start!" Most of the time was spent with the students' sharing their ideas and finding themselves entering naturally into the planning process. Because Howard traveled so extensively, he was often able to identify with the specific locations where people planned to launch their projects and help them take advantage of their unique resources, as well as overcome their unique challenges.

In 1999 Howard collaborated with two others on a book about the leadership and planning principles that were taught and modeled in the PDLS courses. The book was called *Courageous Leaders Transforming Their World,* and his coauthors were James Halcomb and David Hamilton. James Halcomb brought his rich experience in major planning efforts, including the Alaskan pipeline and Apollo space missions, while Howard and David contributed their spiritual perspectives.

The book can be summarized in three main points:

- God-inspired vision: Doing The Right Thing
- God-led plan: Doing Things Right
- God-motivated action: Doing the Right Things Right

Project developers are encouraged to do a five-step leader's plan that includes deciding on an overall objective; "brain writing" end items; laying out milestones; identifying supertasks and subprojects; and evaluating needed resources and critical path. Inspirational insights are woven throughout the pages of the book as expressed in this passage:

> To become the best of leaders we must get to know [God] so intimately that His dreams become our dreams; His vision, our vision; His will, our will. In this way we are not working at cross-purposes with God but are acting as His collaborators. His agenda should shape our agenda; His priorities should impact ours. God's dreams—not just our needs—should be the major influence in defining our vision.

Both the PDLS course and *Courageous Leaders Transforming Their World* have in mind developing-world situations that have limited resources to use in accomplishing the project in mind. The authors drew on the well-known Bible story of Moses and the burning bush to illustrate the attitude of working with the resources at hand. In that encounter, Moses felt inadequate to do what God was calling him to do. Using a simple question, "What is that in your hand?" (Exodus 4:2), God challenged him to consider not what he didn't have but what he did in fact have in his hand, in this case a staff. God helped Moses to use that simple staff to get the attention of the Pharaoh of Egypt and bring about deliverance for His people.

As the authors conclude, "God often asks this question."[1] Just as Howard had often challenged his U of I research teams to work around the inevitable shortages of funding in creative ways, he now showed many U of N teams his positive, can-do perspective.

Over and over in the PDLS setting, Howard and Jim encouraged teams to take what was in their hands and plan boldly. Some project teams overcame their initial hesitation and persevered to success, but not all planning efforts met with the same results. Nevertheless, both men kept to the long and hopeful view.

PDLS was the most obvious, but by no means the only platform from which Howard cast his vision to the upcoming generations of leaders.

MISSION BUILDERS

A second form for helping the work of YWAM and the U of N move forward came from Howard's need to start implementing the master plan that he and Jim Miller had worked on for the Kona campus. Jim had been providing his professional services at no cost. Howard recognized this means of service could be a bridge over which many people could walk to serve God in missions in timely and practical ways. He called these people "Mission Builders" and often told Jim he was the first one.

As Jim relates the story: "Howard was really responsible for getting the Mission Builder program off the ground. He had a high-quality contractor friend in Urbana named Ernie Grothe.

When we were ready for construction, having designed the first building, the "temporary" Administration Building, Howard called his friend and asked if he would come to Kona and be responsible for construction. Ernie came and built that building, still in use after twenty-seven years."

Other leaders followed, including Glen Roper, who managed the sizable volunteer effort in constructing the Global Outreach Center and the first stage of Village 2. Glen had the necessary gifts to coordinate the skills and egos of different contractors who came and gave their time to the projects for months at a time.

One such volunteer was Lynn Batterman, who worked for several years on Kona construction projects. After moving back to the state of Washington, Lynn continued to help with PDLS, teaching base leaders about having a vision and mission statement. Lynn explains: "Vision is to 'see' where the Lord wants to take the ministry—the who, what, why. Mission is to 'do'; it is the action steps that fulfill the vision; it sets out the how, when, where; it sets objectives and measurable goals to meet the objectives."

Howard and then-U of N Kona chancellor, David Boyd, asked Lynn to work with Troy and Jina Stremler of Washington State to start an international Mission Builder program (MBI). The goal was to connect Kona volunteers to service opportunities on other bases and to help YWAM bases begin recruiting their own Mission Builders. Denny Gunderson, the North American director of YWAM, provided guidance.

"Howard was great at encouraging people to use the gifts God had given us to move forward in what God has equipped us to do," Lynn says. "MBI was a great example of that."

Howard often would identify himself as a "mission builder," using his professional talents to further the cause of the mission organization. He never failed to encourage others to do likewise in their own lives.

GENESIS VIDEOCONFERENCING TECHNOLOGY

In the early 1990s Howard was observing the emerging technology of videoconferencing. At that time, mostly businesses and research institutions were experimenting with the capability of seeing and hearing another group of people, thus saving the time and expense of travel.

Howard had foreseen years before the impact this technology could have but was faced with a global university that was slow to appreciate and adopt this new teaching tool. In keeping with his character, he approached the situation gently and with much patience.

In 1994 a group of YWAMers met in Lausanne, Switzerland, to pray about how God could use their base to advance the cause of missions.[2] As they considered the effect that the printing press had on the distribution of Bibles, they began to see that video-conferencing could be used in YWAM as a multiplication tool within core YWAM values. One of the key people in that meeting was Markus Steffen, the first director of what became known as the GENESIS Center in Lausanne. As Markus relates the story, their primary motivation was looking for ways to multiply training to other training centers, allowing a teacher to be heard in many locations at the same time—especially remote locations where it was difficult and expensive for teachers to go.

As the idea grew, an advisory board was formed by Loren to guide the project, and quite naturally he turned to Howard to be one of its directors. Howard brought to this effort not only his vision for the technology but also an unswerving commitment to the core values of YWAM. Markus says he saw in Howard "a man who radiated a soft and gentle spirit, with an ear to listen, a warm smile, and a personality that embraced and accepted others for who they were. Here was a strategic thinker, a big visionary able to make big plans—but always wanting them to be done in God's ways."

Howard called the team together for several weeks of prayer and team interaction as they grappled with the possibilities and priorities. As always for Howard, both parts were essential: prayer and "processing" as a team.

The vision was large: over one thousand training centers linked with videoconferencing capabilities. Again, some wanted to get started quickly if there was any hope of completing the task. Howard was much more interested in hearing everyone's perspectives. He would not "sell" his own points but through interaction allowed the others to draw them out from him. He had the grace to wait for others to receive his input, all the time remaining strong in his convictions.

Howard saw that the foremost value for this project was that YWAM relationships would be strengthened. He wanted remote bases to get the full advantage of the network, giving them both access to the training and a voice in the global YWAM community. As the network grew, he urged that all bases involved move forward at the same pace, not accelerating development where it was easier and slowing down in the hard places.

He was not willing to accept compromise or shortcuts to reach the goal quickly. As he often said, "What starts as temporary becomes permanent." In the same way that one must be patient with a fruit tree, honoring the effects of weather, soil, and other conditions while waiting for the fruit to emerge in due time, he was willing to live with the tension of his enthusiasm being challenged by the approaches of others.

For example, an obvious way to simplify the project would have been to make it a one-way broadcast rather than two-way communications. After all, wasn't the main point to simply let the teacher be heard in far-flung locations? If students had questions, why not just let them email or phone their questions to the teacher? Howard saw clearly the far superior benefit of allowing the teacher and students to "see each other's eyes," as Markus puts it, letting the teacher see the students "with tears in their eyes making a comment" rather than merely reading an expressionless email.

In 1995 a group of young people in India gave sacrificially toward this project, and in 1996 two Leadership Training Schools, in Budapest and Lausanne, were linked for several weeks. Lausanne and Restenas, Sweden, became the first permanent GENESIS locations in 1997. As of October 2004 the GENESIS (Global Electronic Network, Educating, Serving and Inspiring Students) network (www.go-genesis.com) activated its fiftieth location. Beyond teaching, it is used at times for "One Voice" simultaneous worship sessions and other collaborative purposes.

While GENESIS still has a long way to go to achieve the vision of 100,000 students served from a thousand locations, Howard's dream is still driving the team. What Howard foresaw has gradually become reality through much prayer, team effort, and sacrificial giving of time, energy, and money.

In this project Howard showed that it is possible to take advantage of cutting-edge technology without losing sight of the core values of the organization. The author had an opportunity to apply this principle while introducing voice mail to the Kona campus in the mid-1990s. Instead of making the whole system automated with voice recordings, the campus operator role was continued to give the human warmth that callers had come to expect.

CURRICULUM DEVELOPMENT

Howard Malmstadt also played a key role in forming a curriculum team that laid the foundation for YWAM's International Christian Schools and for establishing teaching principles in what became the U of N's College of Education.

As the U of N's colleges developed curriculum in their respective disciplines, one challenge they faced was how to package the curriculum in such a way that it could be multiplied and used in many locations. Howard envisioned a center where representatives of the colleges could step out of their daily responsibilities for a season and work on curriculum packages, such as a video and training manual. Here he was taking his "lab course" concepts from the Heath Kit days and applying them to the problem at hand. This center was to serve the colleges, using a publishing-house model that would create an environment where the colleges could not only individually create curriculum products and tools but also have the opportunity to look at cross-disciplinary issues with their colleagues.

Howard asked educator Bob Lichty to be director for this new Center for Curriculum Development, or Educational Resource Center, as it was later known.

The center's charter outlined a threefold mission: to be a catalyst for curriculum "packages" as they were developed; to be encouragers in all academic areas; and to develop a resource base of editors, illustrators, photographers, and other publishing personnel.

The center would then organize "publishing groups," each including people with various skills and ministry gifts. Howard never stopped preaching the value of the team approach. In addition to helping with curriculum design, the center served the U of N colleges by discovering and bringing other good resources to be shared across colleges, such as the "Walk Thru the Bible" seminars (www.walkthru.org).

A unique part of Howard's model for the U of N was that it should go beyond the typical concerns of the missions community, such as literacy rates or concerns related to spiritual conversion. His was a far more holistic view, insisting that YWAM pay attention to the whole of the human condition, not just the soul to be saved. In this context, it made perfect sense to study and seek solutions for environmental issues such as ozone depletion, desertification, or poor water quality. If people are living in such conditions, it is not only relevant but also essential to address those needs as part of caring for the whole person: body, soul, and spirit.

From that holistic view came *Target Earth,* a publication in 1989 that Howard saw as the "flagship piece" of the center. The book, edited by Frank Kaleb Jansen, encompassed chapters on a wide range of topics of concern to YWAM and other mission agencies. One of the articles in *Target Earth* was written by Howard himself and would prove to be the seed of another vision: clean drinking water for all people on the earth.

As Barbara Overgaard, project manager for *Target Earth,* puts it, Howard's goal in integration was to "create something new that individually the disciplines would not necessarily produce." Each new piece is meant to be shared far beyond the walls where it was created—to other U of N campuses and to the nations.

The essential elements of the vision for this curriculum center—integration across colleges, multiplying resources across U of N and beyond, benefiting the greatest number of people— continue today in a variety of forms within the U of N structure, although the original vision still awaits fulfillment. Howard helped to shatter the walls that are commonplace in the more traditional academic setting, making way for a much more comprehensive approach.

UNIVERSITY LEADERSHIP

Howard knew the infrastructure required to make a university function properly. He recruited Betty Barnett to be the university Registrar, and she and support staff such as Tom Brook, Linda Connorton, and Derek Chignell worked over the years to register hundreds of U of N schools from around the world, develop a catalog of all the available courses, and maintain transcripts for students taking courses on multiple continents. Howard modeled servant leadership to them, often doing the tedious and thankless editing work required to do such projects well, away from the public view.

Howard was interviewed by Camille Bishop as part of her doctoral thesis on leadership transition.[3] His comments on leadership qualities say much about his perspective. When asked for the most important qualities of leaders, he said:

> More and more, though, I am convinced it should be servant leadership and a real understanding of what that means. Another important quality is foresight....Foresight is really understanding when you make a decision what the implications might be for a year, five years, ten years down the road. And it is one of the major failures of leaders, that they don't have foresight.

Howard recognized the pitfalls of having talented leaders without strong spiritual character. In discussing the U of N's need for future leaders, he said, "We need people who will first of all turn to the Lord...people whose lives are characterized by the nature and character of God. We need to be very, very careful....We need leaders who know what they are talking about, but the number one characteristic is their spiritual depth."

Howard constantly looked for, proclaimed, and drew out the potential in others. David Ross remembers Howard commenting that David's young daughter Frances would be a strong athlete, as she later proved to be. Paulette Triplett exclaims that "he saw more in me than I did!" Thomas Grunder, another person who worked with Howard on PDLS and Community Development schools, remembers that "he has championed me way beyond what I thought I could do."

As a result of his encouraging ways, he not only launched many of his own projects but also helped others work more effectively on their own dreams and visions. He modeled for them daily what it meant to be a multiplier.

IO.

Water for Life

Some people think only intellect counts: knowing how to solve problems, knowing how to get by, knowing how to identify an advantage and seize it. But the functions of intellect are insufficient without courage, love, friendship, compassion, and empathy.

—DEAN KOONTZ

*H*oward *was heading down an escalator in Zurich when he lost his balance. Heedless of his own condition, he clutched his precious cargo to himself as he fell. To his great relief, he had saved the items he carried from damage. He would still be able to demonstrate the water filters. That was all that mattered.*

Howard's life vision—by now closely linked with the U of N's purpose—expanded to include what in Hebrew tradition is called *tikkun olam,* the rebuilding of the world. He constantly spoke of the "two-handed gospel," in which meeting people's physical needs must be integrated with Christians' efforts to meet their spiritual needs.

He became deeply concerned over the pressing need in the world today for clean drinking water. In the 1989 missions atlas *Target Earth,* he wrote an article titled "Fresh Water Crisis," in which he sounded a warning about the necessity of the church's rallying to help the more than two billion people—mostly in developing countries—who drink daily from contaminated water sources. During his global travels, Howard saw that contaminated water caused not only needless loss of life but also incredible losses in productivity, economic instability, and poor quality of life for affected populations.

In calling Christians to action, he frequently quoted the words of Jesus in Matthew 25:35: "I was thirsty and you gave me something to drink," and verse 40: "I tell you the truth, whatever you did for one of the least of these brothers of mine, you did for me." Howard interpreted verse 35 to mean the giving of clean water. His *Target Earth* article says, "When Jesus asked us to give water to the thirsty, he meant pure, healthy water, not contaminated disease-bringing poisonous liquid. Therefore, it is a Christian calling and duty to heal bad water as the prophet Elisha did (2 Kings 2:19–22)."[1]

Approaching the water-quality problem as a compassionate scientist and committed Christian, Howard first prayed for wisdom and then applied his considerable intellect and missionary zeal to finding a solution to this global crisis. Howard recognized that traditional methods for water purification are inadequate for two reasons: some consume precious firewood; others are not fully effective on certain harmful substances or small organisms such as viruses.

The more he studied the problem, the more he came to believe that new purification technology had to be developed. He listed stringent requirements for such a system. It had to be low cost, portable, simple to use, and effective against a wide variety of contaminants and require minimal power and water pressure to operate. Howard then began a search process that spanned nearly three years. During that time many people approached him with what they felt was *the* solution to water purification. In some cases, he would find they believed they had heard from God about the design but had not properly tested their ideas. Howard, while respectful of people's motivations, always graciously insisted on testing and didn't find any ideas that met his critical requirements.

Unbeknownst to Howard, another scientist-turned-missionary had been working hard to find that solution. Rolf Engelhard served as a missionary pilot in the 1980s, and his travels made him keenly aware that bad water was causing premature death in people from developing countries. "In most of these villages, the people would drink from the same rivers and lakes that their animals drank out of. As a result, their drinking water had become severely contaminated with unseen deadly microbes and other contaminates," Rolf said. This revelation birthed a passion that became Rolf's life's mission: "to bring clean water to the world."[2]

Rolf was also inspired through a teaching by Loren Cunningham on the two-handed-gospel concept. In 1990 he and his family moved to Prescott, Arizona, where he devoted his time, energy, and life savings to developing a solution to the quest for pure water.

By 1993 Rolf was reaching the bottom of his funds and was desperate to have his design reviewed. He had tried to contact Howard but to no avail. Howard was on an extensive overseas trip and didn't receive the messages until he got home to Michigan. He was exhausted from his travels, but as he told friends later, "I made the 'mistake' of praying and felt I should go meet him." Rolf was surprised and delighted by Howard's call and suggested they fly to Los Angeles and meet at the airport hotel.

Once Howard saw the design, he was immediately impressed with the elegance of the design specifications and the quality of the performance statistics. Another clue that they had been divinely brought together surfaced when Rolf handed Howard an article on global water needs, crediting the article with inspiring him to create the water purifier. In fact, Rolf had the article as the first page of his mission-statement package. Howard, as usual, listened quietly and did not interrupt. Finally, Rolf asked Howard, "Have you read this article?" Howard's response: "Yes, I've read it; in fact, I wrote it!"

Rolf knew he had found the expert he had been looking for to analyze and improve his design. In later years, Howard could never tell that story without weeping for gratitude that God had confirmed their meeting and subsequent collaboration in such a powerful way.

From that point forward, Howard and others in YWAM worked with Rolf to further enhance the design. Howard disassembled it to the individual parts, seeking to make it more effective, reliable, and adaptable, while still portable. He was keenly aware that parts or supplies needed to be cheap to be of help in the developing world.

For support in this effort Howard turned to Rus Alit, an appropriate-technology expert with World Vision in Indonesia and a regular instructor at U of N, Kona. Rus, a much-in-demand consultant, shared Howard's clean-water vision and had developed many simple water technologies, including a homemade, trickle-fed sand filter that uses gravity and two dollars of locally available materials. YWAM teams are still promoting these sand filters across Southeast Asia with good success, although the filters are not fully effective in some settings, and they are not portable.

Engelhard's initial design, called the Voyager unit, was very effective and innovative, but a key drawback in Howard's mind was that the cost to manufacture it was not under his goal of five hundred dollars. Howard convened a summit in early 2001 of mostly U of N faculty, plus others interested in developing a better water filter, to join with Rus Alit and Rolf Engelhard to improve the design. Their analysis focused on both filter improvements and cost cutting.

The Engelhard design[3] contained two prefilters: a coarse metal screen to remove larger contaminants, then a ceramic filter to remove particles and large organisms. Ultraviolet light both produced and worked with ozone gas to kill all living organisms. Finally, a charcoal filter removed such contaminants as pesticides.

This early version was pressure sensitive. If the water pressure was sufficient, the UV light would come on to produce the ozone. Howard and Rus learned that many users reported they were happy with the purifiers but mentioned casually that the light had never come on. They concluded that these people were essentially using a glorified ceramic and charcoal filter, missing the main benefits of the purifier system. Rolf added a twelve-volt electric pump to solve the pressure problem, thus making the purifier perhaps the most effective system in the world.

Howard acknowledged that the water purifier would be a tremendous blessing at mission bases in developing countries and would help visiting teams from developed nations stay healthy. He also believed it would be ideal for middle-class families in developing nations. However, Rolf and Howard's design still cost about five hundred dollars per unit. While this was many times less than equivalent purification systems, Howard knew this would be prohibitive to families in impoverished parts of the world where five hundred dollars represented their yearly income.

The consensus of the 2001 summit was that they should test the Voyager system in real-world settings. In late August, a multilocation U of N conference in Africa (facilitated by the GENESIS videoconferencing technology) provided an opportunity to distribute dozens of test units to YWAMers working in remote locations with serious water problems. These staff members would be enlisted to test the units in these difficult field settings.

U of N's International Community Development Director Christine Colby and her family were among those testing the units. They helped determine the need for a prefilter, such as a T-shirt, to keep mud from clogging the ceramic filter.

The U of N summit's final day was September 11, 2001. Howard, who had been visiting each of the four conference sites in Africa, was in South Africa that day. As the news of the terrible attacks in New York and Washington, D.C., reached the conference, participants knew their travel plans would be affected as airports shut down around the world. Howard and other U of N leaders got swept up in crisis management, and the distribution of test purifiers became somewhat chaotic. Some purifiers went out before full instructions for feedback could be given. As a result, testing of these units produced spotty field data.

In June 2003 Howard presided over a workshop for people interested in taking the project further; by now, it had been named

"Water for Life." As Loren Cunningham said later, "He could not have been more fulfilled, happy, and joyful as those gathered at King's [Mansion] picked up his passion for pure water and received God-directed strategies for implementation."

The Water for Life team consisted of more than a dozen U of N leaders, including Howard's close friend Derek Chignell and many colleagues from the College of Science & Technology. They began promoting various purification methods, including the Voyager system and rainwater catchments. Team members subsequently taught Pacific Islanders how to build simple concrete tanks to hold rain directed from the roofs of homes and public buildings.

Allan Robbins was part of one Water for Life team that served in the island nation of Kiribati. Working alongside eager islander volunteers, they built four full-size demonstration tanks. Rather than about one thousand dollars for a premade tank, these cost about sixty dollars each. Allan reported, "By the end of our stay, we had trained twenty islanders to build these eight-hundred-gallon rain containment tanks, and one village elder was so excited he committed to help each household in his village build a tank so that every family could have sufficient, safe drinking water."

Rus Alit also was spreading the Water for Life vision, inventing and improving technologies to supply clean water for people in developing nations. His simple ram pump, sand filters, and cisterns have improved the quality of life for many villages in Southeast Asia. He continues to teach these technologies at an annual Water Technologies seminar at the U of N, Kona. (For details go to www.uofnkona.edu/sat/techseminars.html.)

While others around him were pushing for wider distribution of the water purifiers, Howard urged a more cautious approach. He believed the design was in good shape, but he was concerned about maintenance. He believed that a poorly maintained water purifier, lulling its users into a false sense of security, was in fact worse than no purifier at all. He also was resistant to an entrepreneurial approach to distribution, preferring a model of "giving and receiving."

The Vortex Voyager unit, as it is now called, is currently marketed within the United States (www.vortexwater.com). One distribution channel is being managed by Joe Hurston, a Christian businessman in Florida. Through his Airmobile Ministries (www.airmobile.org), he places the units in disaster-relief situations. Notably, Airmobile Ministries distributed a number of units to missionaries and health-service workers in Indonesia during the ongoing relief effort following the devastating December 2004 tsunami.

Now good friends, Joe and Rolf have more than the water purifier in common: both are pilots, both are entrepreneurs, and both have a vision for missions. They have participated in televised events to demonstrate the amazing effectiveness of the unit. For example, in Haiti they stood in flood waters containing garbage and corpses; right next to a floating donkey corpse, they stuck the Voyager intake tube into the water, turned it on, and proceeded to drink glass after glass of the purified water as the cameras rolled.

Their desire is to see the units used much more extensively in third-world situations, both by relief workers for their own protection, by people trapped in chronic water-quality problems, and by victims of natural disasters.

The Water for Life team continues to work on maintaining Vortex water purifiers in the locations where they were installed in 2001, and the Water for Life Initiative continues to be an active part of the Malmstadt legacy. Its mission statement reads in part: "Water for Life exists to help people develop safe and sustainable water sources for their communities."

As the Water for Life home page (www.waterforlife.org) states, "Dr. Malmstadt's vision continues to influence the Water for Life team. This team reflects people from many different backgrounds and nationalities, all committed to using their skills to help individuals and communities have access to safe water."

The seeds planted by Howard in his *Target Earth* article have found fertile ground, and his far-reaching ideas have experienced a degree of practical expression. However, the full promise of his vision for pure water remains unfulfilled.

Howard's leadership on this project showed his determination to benefit even the poorest people through technology. He demonstrated perseverance in seeking the best solution to the problem of pure water and the principle of generosity when it came to the issue of marketing and distribution. This project perhaps best portrays his belief that the pursuit of science is meant to help others as an essential part of reaching them with the message of the Christian gospel.

II.

Homecoming

All of life is a coming home. Salesmen, secretaries, coal miners,
beekeepers, sword swallowers, all of us. All the restless hearts of
the world, all trying to find a way home.

— PATCH ADAMS

*I*t was 1998, and Howard was attending a YWAM conference in
Brazil. He had been plagued with skin cancers for some time, and
anticipated surgery on his ear when he returned to Kona. However, par-
ticipants of the conference gathered around their dear Howard to pray for
healing for his ear.

When Howard returned to Kona, a College of Counseling and Health
Care staff member inspected his ear and marveled that the skin was as
smooth and flexible as a baby's. No surgery was necessary.

Howard knew the healing had been a miracle.

Howard suffered from an increasing assortment of health
problems in his latter years, but he rarely spoke of them to friends
and colleagues, and he kept working to rally support for expansion
of U of N International.

He also suffered a series of transient and intermittent strokes,
with a major one in Florida in 1997, when he was rushed to the
hospital. Afterward, he disregarded doctors' orders about travel
and flew home. This incident led to more serious medical problems

and continued strokes. Linda Connorton, his academic assistant in Kona, recalls one incident in which he passed out and fell backward on the stairs leading to his room. Linda, who was walking behind him, broke his fall, and both of them suffered bruises. On another occasion in 2002, Derek Chignell discovered that Howard had fallen in the bathtub, unable to get out for twenty-four hours. Derek tried unsuccessfully to persuade Howard to receive medical attention. The next day Betty Barnett and infectious-disease specialist Allan Robbins finally prevailed on him to let Allan examine him; they found bruises and infection throughout his body. Only then did Howard consent to get medical help. It was good that he had persistent friends to push through such self-defeating stubbornness.

Howard returned to Carolyn in Michigan in mid-December 2002, then came back to Kona in February 2003 in time for his eighty-first birthday, which he celebrated in small gatherings with friends. He was still weak and unsteady on his feet when he traveled back to Michigan at the end of February. Two months of rest and home cooking reenergized him. When he returned to Kona in May, friends remarked at how much healthier he looked.

From June 3 to 12, he led a Water for Life workshop. Participants came together to seek the Lord and do strategic planning for developing, testing, and distributing the water-purifier kits. Although Howard had been careful to take an hour-long nap each day of the workshop, he admitted afterward that he felt tired, a physical fatigue that clung to him every day thereafter. Nevertheless, in the weeks that followed he enjoyed a series of meals with small groups of friends, including his assistants Linda Connorton and Derek Chignell, his veterinarian friend John Kuhne—whom he often called "my doctor"—and David Ross and Jim Miller at the Ross home on Father's Day.

Later in June, Howard was able to speak on "Pure Water for Missions" as part of the Humanities and Science core course at the U of N. As Derek relates, "If you had been there, you would have heard some of the things that were always a part of his teaching, like this: 'How well you listen and respond could be a matter of life and death.' Or this, 'In all the plans we make, we must listen to the voice of the Lord. If you haven't heard from the Lord—if you haven't got His vision—then your plans are no plans at all.' And this, 'I believe in the two-handed gospel with water. This means giving pure water, coupled with the Living Water. Never one without the other!' And then this, 'Always, always move in unity—together!'"

Prior to teaching the first day, a Wednesday, Howard prayed that the students would be responsive to his instruction. In his experience of teaching at the U of N, the international students who came under his teaching were often overwhelmed with the breadth and depth of his knowledge, on top of the language and cultural barriers. At first, he was disappointed at the lack of feedback and classroom interaction. About an hour into the teaching session he fainted, and paramedics were called. They ruled out a heart attack but wanted to take him to the hospital for observation. Howard declined to go, insisting on teaching the rest of the afternoon from a chair. The students' attention was riveted by all he had to say, and, indeed, he spoke prophetically and powerfully.

This incident made a profound impact on the students and Howard's friends who gathered around him in concern. It certainly got the attention of the class—in fact, Howard claimed this as an answer to his prayers. Derek reminded him that this particular technique should not be used more than once!

The diagnosis was simple anemia, and true to form Howard taught the class the next day as well, assisted by Jeff Waddell and Derek Chignell. His Kona doctor was trying to reach him to discuss a blood transfusion and had Linda deliver that message to him. Howard took one look at the note and said, "That's what I thought." Likely, he knew his own condition even better than the doctor did, but nevertheless he refused to go to the hospital for the procedure.

Derek describes the scene on the last day of the class, when they prayed about how to respond to Howard's message. First, they felt they should pray for the Water for Life team—for wisdom, strength, direction, finances, and clear communication. This led them to more personal prayers, as Derek tells the story: "'Open our hearts and remove the stone covering the wells in our lives and release the water of life!' and 'We repent for the apathy of our generation, and we commit again to be the Howard generation, and we will do it! We will be multigenerational!' A question was asked: 'If Howard were not here, would we continue lining up with God's intention for University of the Nations?' The response from the rest of the class was 'Yes, yes we would!'"

There was then a word from Howard, and this is what he said: "In prayer, I feel this class is very special, not just for water, but for many other things as well." The class then gathered around Howard to minister to him. Two students knelt at his feet and said, "We have grown up with you over many years in this mission, and you reflect more of the character of Jesus than anyone else we know." And then a beautiful Korean song was sung by one student—"You are a channel of blessing and God's covenant. Through you all the nations come back to God."

On Friday, the fourth of July, Howard had breakfast with Jim and Gwen Beeby. Over the weekend he had visits from old friends Dean and Carol Beaumont, Ross and Margaret Tooley, and Yolanda and Roxanne Olson.

That Sunday, before leaving church, he declared to Pastor Stan Harbour, "I am going home tomorrow!" Although he was feeling very tired, he had enough energy to take some friends out for lunch, having a veggie sandwich capped with a favorite dessert—carrot cake. His conversation after lunch was filled with near- and far-term plans: the U of N Synergy workshop in Singapore that fall, the Water for Life project, plans for King's Mansion, and his eagerness to return home to Carolyn after a six-week separation.

Since he was on campus that Sunday evening (July 6), Howard would normally have delighted in going through the food line and engaging folks in conversation over the meal. However, his tiredness caused him to stay in his room and request a special treat from a friend: a McDonald's fish filet sandwich and a chocolate milkshake. Derek comments: "He was always a little sheepish about asking for that, since it isn't the healthiest of meals."

Howard's plan was to rest once he was home in Michigan prior to going to Singapore in August. He had tried to get adequate rest in Kona, but he kept pouring out his energies. As Yolanda Olson commented, "A young man would have had a hard time duplicating his schedule during that time." His schedule included an interview for a CD, another one for public-access TV, leading a seminar, writing two reports, a teaching time, and on-campus devotionals. Howard also attended public worship services and many one-on-one and group meetings.

That Sunday afternoon, he told his colleague Linda Connorton that he would need a wheelchair to get on the plane the next day. He said he didn't think he could manage the stairs from the tarmac into the plane. Linda and Derek were concerned about the implications of that first-ever request, so they supplemented it by bringing someone to drive Linda and Howard to the airport. They also arranged for a wheelchair at Howard's San Francisco stopover and alerted Jon to drive to the airport in Chicago to minimize the strain on that end of the journey.

That evening, Yolanda and Roxanne Olson dropped by to help him clean his room and deliver some final laundry items—including a much-loved aloha shirt he had received on his birthday. He insisted they just talk rather than clean. He napped at one point, giving them an opportunity to do some quick cleaning, and he awakened disoriented for a few moments. As they were leaving, Yolanda reminded him they were going to the weekly prayer at the Plaza of the Nations. "I asked him if he had any specific prayer needs we could pray for," Yolanda recalls. "He said, 'Oh yes! Please pray for this Water for Life project, that it will really get off the ground!' Then I asked, 'But Dr. Malmstadt, how about you? Do you have any personal prayer needs?' He said, 'No, I'm fine. Everything's fine!' I said, "Then we will just pray that you will have a good trip home...and strength for the journey." As they said goodbye, Howard smiled and gave them each a big, farewell hug. When Jeff Waddell came later that evening to pack the water-purifier units, Howard insisted on packing his suitcase himself so he would know where everything was. When Jeff bid him farewell, he had no inkling that he would be the last person to see Howard alive.

Derek came by the next morning, July 7, and knocked on Howard's door. When he got no answer, he was a little concerned but thought Howard might still be out at breakfast with Loren. Linda arrived a little later, prompted by a call from Carolyn, who was worried that she had not received her usual preflight call from Howard. Linda also got no answer to her knock on his door. She had a key and was the first to find him lying peacefully on his bed with a faint smile on his face. She and Derek arranged for him to be taken to the Kona hospital, where he was pronounced dead.

Derek called Carolyn to confirm their worst fears. Carolyn's response was "Praise the Lord, he's home." Linda and Derek finally got through to daughter Cynthia in Switzerland and son-in-law Tom Bloomer in Australia. Within hours, the news spread through the YWAM world, although the Kona campus community meeting that Wednesday received the first public announcement of Howard's "homecoming." Throughout the crowd there were tear-streaked faces and shouts of praise for the life of this great man. At that meeting there was an outpouring of dedication to God and His purposes. "Many youth and others were giving themselves to God in a fresh way for missions," Derek says.

Carolyn was mercifully spared the days of hectic preparation that week. Tom and Cynthia arrived in time for the Thursday memorial service, but Carolyn's luggage didn't, and she had to borrow clothes for the event. Hundreds crowded around the Plaza of the Nations as a spectacular Kona sunset shone on them. The multinational flags stood at half-mast around the plaza as a clear reminder that Howard's departure was being felt by all the nations of the world, as he had invested so much in so many. The memorial program and web site overflowed with tributes, and dozens of colleagues, friends, and family members spoke on that glorious evening of July 10, 2003, celebrating the life of the Lord Jesus in Howard Malmstadt. The evening's theme was based on 2 Samuel 3:38: "Do you not realize that a prince and a great man has fallen this day?"

Loren Cunningham gave this tribute to his dear friend:

Dr. Howard V. Malmstadt was…a son, a husband, a father, a grandfather, a scholar, a naval officer, a scientist, a university professor of renown, a mentor of scientists, an advisor to U.S. presidents, cofounder of the University of the Nations, founder of the U of N College of Science and Technology, founding provost of the U of N, international chancellor of the U of N…and a good friend to many. But most of all, he was a mighty man of God—a man after God's own heart—who humbly served and wisely counseled others in the ways of God.…

The great loss we feel is only in the human sense, for Howard is with the Lord, and the Lord is with us. We thank God for the gift of Howard's life and his investment into each of our lives as we have colabored together for the kingdom of God.

Margaret Tooley, who with her husband, Ross, has served for decades with YWAM, said of their dear friend:

Howard was not just the father of the University of the Nations—he was the living laboratory of its values and ideas, which he embodied so magnificently. His gifts and accomplishments equipped him to sit among the high elite—but he chose to sit with us—with me!—encouraging, explaining (again), sharing, caring, giving of himself as though his strength and time, energy and love had no limit and no end.

The sadness that day was real, yet not crushing, given the awareness of those present that their loss was heaven's gain. Derek Chignell's moving tribute closed with these words:

This man Howard, who worked in spectroscopy, the study of light, is now living in the presence of pure light, the

Light of God! This man who had a passion for water is now drinking freely of the Water of Life! This man who was a father to so many is now experiencing the full extent of his heavenly Father's welcome.... We will miss you, but we will rejoice in the memory of a life lived to the fullest—and lived well!

Howard's daughter Cynthia Bloomer and her husband, Tom, both gave moving tributes to Howard as a godly father and mentor. Then Loren called all present to rededicate themselves to the God Howard served throughout his life. He also drew attention to a note in the program that read, "In honor of Dr. Howard V. Malmstadt's high regard for ice cream, fellowship over ice cream will ensue at the end of the service."

The family hosted a smaller memorial service in Michigan on July 15, and the Synergy U of N conference in Singapore a few months later dedicated a portion of the program to honoring Howard's memory. Howard's own family was surprised at the memorial services to hear of his many accomplishments . As his widow, Carolyn, puts it, his family knew he was busy and that his travels took him to many countries, but even they were largely ignorant of how wide and deep his impact had been. At home, as everywhere else in his life, Howard Malmstadt had been reticent to speak of himself.

A few days after the Kona memorial service, a few close friends gathered at the West Hawaii Veterans Cemetery, where they carried Howard's flag-draped coffin and laid his body to rest in a simple plot. After all the years of travel, Howard was buried close to his beloved Kona campus, alongside fellow navy war veterans.

Allan Robbins recalls the reaction of some navy veterans who observed the ceremony with tears in their eyes. One of them exclaimed, "We can't believe that such a man lived here among us!" Yolanda adds, "Loren was obviously in mourning, but at one point, when he saw the veterans who had come to do military protocol, he laid aside his grief and spoke to them of the Lord that Howard Malmstadt served and loved." Carolyn, although unable to come because of poor health, had agreed with the choice of burial location. After all, as she explained, "I know where he is—he is with the Lord!"[1]

12.

The Malmstadt Legacy

Whatever you have learned or received or heard from me, or seen in me—put it into practice.

— PHILIPPIANS 4:9

Follow my example, as I follow the example of Christ.

— I CORINTHIANS 11:1

*H*oward had a personal copy of the classic devotional by Oswald Chambers, *My Utmost for His Highest*. He didn't make many marks in the book, but he did underline part of the following passage:

> When looking back on the lives of men and women of God the tendency is to say—What wonderfully astute wisdom they had! How perfectly they understood all God wanted! The astute mind behind is the Mind of God, not human wisdom at all. We give credit to human wisdom when we should give credit to the Divine guidance of God through childlike people who were foolish enough to trust God's wisdom and the supernatural equipment of God.[1]

As Carolyn points out, this passage "describes very profoundly Howard's point of view."

How can one describe the legacy of Dr. Howard V. Malm-stadt? It may be impossible to assess because it reaches so far and wide, overlapping the fields of wartime service, science, education, and missions on a global scale. It continues to grow because so many touched by his life see themselves as having the "privilege" to carry that legacy forward.

Of course, laboratory colleagues would say that Howard's primary legacy is scientific and that it continues to this day. No doubt, Howard will be remembered as one of the great synthesizers of the twentieth century. Scientific growth spurts often happen where two apparently unrelated disciplines interface. For example, the discovery of DNA's structure came about when physicists crossed disciplines and looked at the field of biology. Howard's great contribution to scientific discovery came through his combining the fields of electronics and chemistry. As his long-time friend and colleague Derek Chignell explains, "Howard found himself at the right time and place when the digital revolution was happening. Whereas analytical chemistry had long been focused on weighing and measuring, Howard helped the new field of instrumental chemistry to emerge as an area of study on its own."

Today, Howard's work affects the average person through a wide range of clinical and industrial diagnostics. For example, we now take for granted fast and accurate results for blood tests, thanks in large part to digitally controlled instrumentation that Howard and his students helped pioneer.

Howard predicted that personal computers would one day supersede the huge industrial/corporate computers of his day. As others developed microchips, Howard and his students incorporated them into the instruments they were designing. He had a genius for applying discoveries from other scientific fields to advance the work of analytical chemistry and spectroscopy.

Howard's key insight into instrumentation was that many of the devices being invented consisted of the same basic modules. By recombining these building blocks in various ways, different instruments could be made quickly and cheaply. This concept helped in teaching students, as Howard showed them how to enhance existing instruments to solve new laboratory problems.

Another part of the Malmstadt legacy is his passion for the study of light. Analytical chemistry, in particular spectroscopy, analyzes the qualities of light as it passes through various compounds. Howard developed much of the early instrumentation used for spectroscopic analysis. In honoring his work, scientific colleagues said Howard's pioneering research advanced the entire field of spectroscopy.

Howard told friends he wanted to write a book on light, and some encouraged him to write one that could be read and understood by the layperson. Sadly, he never did write such a book. In the last days of his life, he spoke of wanting to learn even more about light as a means of understanding energy in general. For one who accomplished a great deal, the fact is he dreamed even more. As a result, he constantly lived with the regret of unmet goals.

Howard's interest in light went beyond the merely scientific. Paulette Triplett recalls a devotional Howard gave in the U of N's Arts Foundation School in 2001. The talk was about the role of light in art. Howard described how little we perceive with the naked eye of colors and the full spectrum of light. His Urbana pastor, Dick Foth, recalls that he used to pump Howard for insights on the dual nature of light—as a wave and as a particle. From these insights Dick derived sermons on the multifold character of God. For Howard, the study and appreciation of light led naturally to the study and worship of the Author of Light.

Markus Steffen, who worked with him on U of N's multimedia GENESIS project, says part of Howard's legacy is the way he modeled Christlike interdependence. "Howard knew his own strengths and limitations. For example, he knew he was not particularly gifted as a speaker and preacher; for that part of the work, he relied on Loren." Howard's relationship with Loren showed his keen awareness of his need for others. In the leadership of the U of N, he was content to be the "brain," covered by the "head." Markus says, "Howard didn't just persuade others to practice interdependence; he modeled it in his own life in many ways." Howard's style was the antithesis of today's "networking," in which contacts are exploited to one's own advantage. He expressed genuine love regardless of who the other person was or how "useful" he or she might be to him later on.

In her book *Real Power: Stages of Personal Power in Organizations,* Janet Hagberg identifies six stages of leadership, culminating in "stage 6" leaders, who lead from "behind."[2] Very few leaders have achieved that stage more effectively than Howard. When in YWAM or U of N conferences, he shunned the front rows, preferring to be in the middle or back, mingling with people and drawing them out.

Camille Bishop quotes Howard as saying, "I function by identifying what needs to be done, explain why, and let the people pick up on it. I make suggestions along the way and see if they pick up on them. That is one of the ways of seeing if you have people who are capable of moving into leadership; they really pick up on things."[3]

She believes the most important thing future generations can learn from Howard's life is the importance of Christlike character:

> Central to that was Howard's commitment to the poor and needy...not just a vague concern for the nations of the world. He was not swayed by money, status or power in others or for himself. He was a humble servant, very approachable; without those qualities, one cannot truly disciple nations.
>
> Howard's philosophy of education is so important to continue. He believed we need both education and missionary zeal. His method was to study diligently, then to use it for the sake of God's kingdom. There are two common errors made with respect to education: one is to focus too much on the theoretical, in the process becoming irrelevant to real-world problems. The other is to dash off with limited knowledge and preparation, possibly doing more harm than good. Howard stood for a healthy balance of the two. He was truly a man of excellence.[4]

Ed Sherman, the acting international dean of U of N's College of Humanities and International Studies, came to understand the depth of that excellence only after Howard's death. While Ed had enormous respect for Howard's character and devotion to God, he had for years wondered if Howard had missed God's will in coming to the U of N. "In my spirit, I took offense at Howard's life. I thought how could someone waste such a spectacular career, with influence reaching across the world?...He was already discipling the nations....How could he walk away from the opportunities for more breakthrough discoveries, helping to improve the lives of countless people...only to come to a Podunk university in the Pacific?"

For Ed, revelation came as he sat with many others at the YWAM Synergy conference in Singapore a few months after Howard's death. Listening to Tom Bloomer speak of Howard's "crucified excellence," he began to understand what Howard had meant the U of N to become: "not an ivory tower, separating its theory from practice, but integrated into the life of the world, and intimately involved in transforming the world." Howard knew that there was only one way that would happen—if people hold on to excellence and yet crucify it; that is, lay down the trappings of reputation and position. In Howard's case Ed saw that "he crucified that reputation, he crucified that position" and came to a place where he was an unknown, simply "Howard."

The result for Ed was that Tom's comment opened his eyes that the U of N is "doing something that's never been done before," and this gave him a whole new sense of excitement to be a part of carrying on Howard's vision. Ed also came to realize that he had been like the disciples who took offense at the extravagance of the woman who poured expensive perfume on the head of Jesus (Matthew 26:6–13). Jesus said to them, "I tell you the truth, wherever this gospel is preached throughout the world, what she has done will also be told, in memory of her." No doubt Howard's extravagant "gift" will also be spoken of for generations to come.

YWAMers throughout the world still speak often of Howard Malmstadt. Anna Colby tells of how "Uncle Howard" pulled her aside amid the fear and turmoil of September 11, 2001, and explained in terms the eleven-year-old could understand just how much the world had changed in a single day. Her last time with Howard was going to an ice-cream shop together. "When I think about trying to be like him, my desire is to serve God with all my heart."

Douglas Feaver remembers a valuable lesson he learned from Howard. The Kona campus had just hosted an extravagant celebration of Douglas's seventy-fifth birthday. Afterward, he and his wife, Margaret, met with Howard, as they often did when he was in town. Douglas recalls:

> We shared with Howard our sense of being so overwhelmed by the magnitude of the event, with its honors and affirmations, and so unworthy of it all. He put our hearts at rest out of his own experience of receiving recognition and rewards. Howard told us, "Just remember, as those who love and serve the Lord, such honor is but a reflection of His life in you. It acknowledges His blessing upon you."
>
> We have never forgotten Howard's words of wisdom. His perspective showed us how to accept honor in the spirit of humility and grace. It was a key to his own life.

Loren Cunningham often speaks of Howard's hunger for learning as an important part of his legacy. "Howard was always learning, up until his last day on earth."

Donna Livingston tells of Howard and Carolyn's lifelong practice of looking for those losing hope in themselves, and finding ways to encourage them to carry on. Donna says she wants to continue that mission in her own life.

Allan Robbins spoke of his mentor Howard on Memorial Day weekend in 2004, when he took a Boy Scout troop to a community ceremony at West Hawaii Veterans Cemetery. Speeches in honor of the fallen veterans helped the boys to see the significance of each life. Allan then took them to Howard's grave and highlighted the importance of his life and the places God had called him to.

Another person who speaks continually of Howard Malmstadt

is Paul Dangtoumbda, Howard's protégé and a pioneer of U of N campuses in Togo and Nigeria. At a YWAM event in New Zealand that turned out to be their last face-to-face meeting, Howard prayed for his beloved disciple, wrapping him in a warm embrace as Paul wept and experienced God's healing touch.

Months later, Paul was on a ministry trip in Africa and stopped at an Internet café to check his email. One of those emails contained the terrible news that Howard had died. Overcome with grief, he wept uncontrollably, wandering aimlessly on the street. He eventually found himself in a restaurant, where the scents of illegal drugs pierced the fog of his sorrow. Paul suddenly came to realize he was sitting in a gangster hangout. Drug dealers at tables nearby eyed him suspiciously, thinking he was there invading their territory. One came over and questioned who he was and what he was doing there. When Paul explained that he was a missionary and was mourning the loss of his spiritual father, the gang leader pressed him for more information.

Paul began to share the gospel with the man and spoke of Howard's influence on his life. Right there in front of his fellow gang members, the man began to spill out his story of criminal activity, including murdering many people, dealing in illegal drugs, stealing from ships, and running from the police. He asked Paul to pray for him that he would not go back to that life, and he requested a Bible. Paul was happy to oblige.

When it was time to go, the gang leader ordered his men to escort Paul to the bus and carry his suitcase. "Don't touch this man," he told them. As Paul put it, "God knew what He was doing in bringing me into that situation." Even in death, Howard's practice of valuing and caring for people was bringing new life. Paul Dangtoumbda continues to apply those lessons as he designs and builds U of N campuses in Africa.

Second-generation YWAMer Troy Sherman laments that Howard remains an unknown hero to many touched by his legacy:

> Hundreds around the world have stepped from darkness into the light...through the obedience of this man. Every degree student in the University of the Nations who walks

away with a revelation of God...each African given the chance for an education that they never had before...every street child saved by U of N students...every child and family still alive because of pure water from Howard's water filter...is a testimony of Howard's greatness. He has blessed lives of people he never met, but those who met him are the most blessed.

Diagnosed early in life with attention deficit disorder, Troy felt doomed to failure in traditional education. At the U of N, he experienced a new sense of freedom. He said, "I became free to run with the Author of wisdom. My self-confidence was transformed." He went on to complete a BA in Christian ministries with high grades throughout. Troy said, "I found a university that believed in me when I did not believe in myself, that cared more about who I could become than how much I could pay, that believed I could honestly change the world. I found a university like Howard Malmstadt."

Howard taught in several of the YWAM courses Troy attended as a student. The last one had the most impact on Troy. Howard strayed from the topic at hand and "began to speak from something deep within him: a heart cry for a legacy, a heart cry for the dream of the University of the Nations to go on long after he passed on. You could see in his eyes that he knew his time was short, and in midsentence he collapsed to the floor. By the time the paramedics arrived, my wife, Alisa, and I were holding his head in our laps. His eyes opened, and as always his smile lit up the room."

Instead of thinking of his own condition, Howard had them promise that Jesus would remain the focus of the U of N. With tears Troy and the others vowed to uphold that promise. After Howard passed away, Troy came to realize that he "had been walking in the shadow of a great man...that he himself was a small part of an incredible legacy that had just begun."

Afterword

Of all the lessons we can learn from Howard Malmstadt, which is most important? Perhaps this: that we need not choose between a life lived in pursuit of God and a life lived in pursuit of excellence in our work. Howard showed that we can do both, and we can do both with all our hearts and strength to the very end of our lives.

This is "the most excellent way" that the apostle Paul spoke of in 1 Corinthians 12:31—the way of true Christian love. Let us follow Howard on this way—into the light, into the nations, and finally into the eternal presence of God.

Key Articles and Books by Howard Malmstadt

TECHNICAL ARTICLES

"An Automatic Differential Potentiometric Titrator." With E. R. Fett. *Analytical Chemistry* 26 (1954): 1348.

"Automatic Spectrophotometric Titrations." With E. C. Gohrbandt. *Analytical Chemistry* 26 (1954): 442.

"Emission Spectrochemical Analysis of Vanadium and Iron in Titanium Tetrachloride. Spark-in-Spray Excitation." With R. G. Scholz. *Analytical Chemistry* 27 (1955): 881.

"Automatic Derivative Spectrophotometric Titrations." With C. B. Roberts. *Analytical Chemistry* 28 (1956): 1408.

"Precision Null-Point Potentiometry. A Simple, Rapid and Accurate Method for Low Concentration Chloride Determinations." With J. D. Winefordner. *Anal. Chim. Acta* 20 (1959): 283.

"Determination of Glucose in Blood Serum by a New, Rapid, and Specific Automatic System." With G. P. Hicks. *Analytical Chemistry* 32 (1960): 394.

"Precision Null-Point Atomic Absorption Spectrochemical Analysis." With W. E. Chambers. *Analytical Chemistry* 32 (1960): 225.

"Emission Characteristics and Sensitivity in a High-Voltage Spark Discharge." With J. P. Walters. *Analytical Chemistry* 37 (1965): 1484.

"Unique System for Studying Flame Spectrometric Processes."
With G. M. Hieftje. *Analytical Chemistry* 40 (1968): 1860.

"Q-Switched Laser Energy Absorption in the Plume of an Aluminum Alloy." With E. H. Piepmeier. *Analytical Chemistry* 41 (1969): 700.

"Tunable Organic Dye Laser as an Excitation Source for Atomic Flame Fluorescence Spectroscopy." With M. B. Denton. *Appl. Phys. Lett.* 18 (1971): 485.

"Photon Counting for Spectrophotometry." With M. L. Franklin and G. Horlick. *Analytical Chemistry* 44 (1972): 63A.

"Programmable Power Supply for Operation of Hollow Cathode Lamps in an Intermittent Current-Regulated High Intensity Mode." With E. Cordos. *Analytical Chemistry* 44 (1972): 2407.

"Automated Stopped-Flow Analyzer in Clinical Chemistry: Determination of Albumin with Bromcresol Green and Purple." With M. A. Koupparis and E. P. Diamandis. *Clin. Chim. Acta* 149 (1985): 225.

TECHNICAL BOOKS

Electronics for Scientists. With C. G. Enke. New York: W. A. Benjamin, 1963.

Digital Electronics for Scientists. With C. G. Enke. New York: W. A. Benjamin, 1969.

Computer Logic. With C. G. Enke. New York: W. A. Benjamin, 1970.

Electronic Measurements for Scientists. With C. G. Enke and S. R. Crouch. Menlo Park, Calif.: W. A. Benjamin, 1973.

Experiments in Digital and Analog Electronics (ADDbook ONE). With C. G. Enke and S. R. Crouch. Derby, Conn.: E&L Instruments, 1977.

Electronics and Instrumentation for Scientists. With C. G. Enke and S. R. Crouch. Reading, Mass.: Benjamin/Cummings, 1981.

Laboratory Electronics: Hands-On. With C. G. Enke and S. R. Crouch. Washington, D.C.: American Chemical Society, 1984.

Microcomputers and Electronic Instrumentation: Making the Right Connections. With C. G. Enke and S. R. Crouch. Washington, D.C.: American Chemical Society, 1994.

NONTECHNICAL ARTICLES AND BOOKS

"Fresh Water Crisis." In *Target Earth: The Necessity of Diversity in a Holistic Perspective on World Mission.* Edited by Frank Kaleb Jansen. Kailua-Kona: University of the Nations and Global Mapping International, 1989.

Courageous Leaders Transforming Their World. With James Halcomb and David Hamilton. Seattle: YWAM Publishing, 1999.

Notes

CHAPTER 1

[1] "A Tribute to Howard Malmstadt," *Online Magazine*, September 1994, http://www.uofnkona.edu/Father.html.

CHAPTER 2

[1] R.R. Keene, "WWII: 60 Years Ago: Saipan-'Please Apologize Deeply to the Emperor'," *Leatherneck Magazine*, June 2004, http://www.mca-marines.org/Leatherneck.

[2] David Moore, Cdr. USN (Ret.), "The Battle of Saipan: The Final Curtain," 2002, http://www.battleofsaipan.com/seabee.htm.

[3] Naval Historical Center, "US Navy and Marine Corps Personnel Casualties in World War II," http://www.history.navy.mil/faqs/faq11-1.htm.

[4] William Mosher, *USS Wilkes: The Lucky Ship* (Franklin, S.C.: Geneology Publishing Services, 1997).

[5] Mary T. Vreeland, "U of N's Visionary Father," *Online Magazine*, 1994, http://www.uofnkona.edu/Father.html.

CHAPTER 3

The epigraph to this chapter is drawn from *Leadership Jazz* by Max De Pree (New York: Dell, 1992). This was one of Howard's favorite books.

[1] "Atomic Absorption Spectroscopy 1952–77," Australian Academy of Science, http://www.science.org.au/academy/memoirs/walsh2.htm#8.

[2] American Society for Mass Spectrometry, "What Is Mass Spectrometry?" http://www.asms.org/whatisms/p1.html.

[3] James Halcomb, David Hamilton, and Howard Malmstadt, *Courageous Leaders Transforming Their World* (Seattle: YWAM Publishing, 1999), 54.

CHAPTER 4

[1] Newsletter of the Analytical Division of the American Chemical Society, Spring 1992, http://www.acs-analytical.duq.edu.

CHAPTER 5

The epigraph to this chapter is drawn from James Halcomb, David Hamilton, and Howard Malmstadt, *Courageous Leaders Transforming Their World* (Seattle: YWAM Publishing, 1999), 210.

[1] Halcomb, Hamilton, and Malmstadt, *Courageous Leaders*, 187.

[2] S. R. Crouch, et al., "Our Remembrances of Howard Malmstadt," *Applied Spectroscopy* vol. 58, no. 6 (2004), 165–72.

CHAPTER 6

[1] "A Tribute to Howard Malmstadt."

[2] Halcomb, Hamilton, and Malmstadt, *Courageous Leaders*, 92.

[3] Matthew 28:18–20.

[4] This and, unless otherwise noted, the other quotations from here to the end of the chapter are from "A Tribute to Howard Malmstadt."

CHAPTER 7

[1] Until mentioned otherwise in the text, all quotes in this section are from the 1986 U of N Campus Development Guide.

[2] University of the Nations Annual Report, 2003, p. 3.

[3] http://www.uofnkona.edu/History.html.

[4] Camille Bishop, "Generational Cohorts and Cultural Diversity as Factors Affecting Leadership Transition in Organizations" (PhD thesis, Trinity Evangelical Divinity School, May 2004).

CHAPTER 9

[1] Halcomb, Hamilton, and Malmstadt, *Courageous Leaders*, 184.

[2] Marjon Busstra and Erin Reep, "GENESIS Links Students, and Africa," http://www.ywam.org/articles/article.asp?AID=161.

[3] Camille Bishop, "Generational Cohorts and Cultural Diversity as Factors Affecting Leadership Transition in Organizations" (PhD thesis, Trinity Evangelical Divinity School, May 2004).

CHAPTER 10

[1] Howard Malmstadt, "Fresh Water Crisis," in *Target Earth: The Necessity of Diversity in a Holistic Perspective on World Mission*, gen. ed. Frank Kaleb Jansen (Kailua Kona: University of the Nations and Global Mapping International, 1989), 38.

[2] Lila Smith, "The Inventor's Story," http://www.vortexpluswater.com/inventor.htm.

[3] http://www.vortexwater.com/emergency.htm

CHAPTER 11

The epigraph to this chapter is drawn from the film *Patch Adams* (Universal Studios, 1998), directed by Tom Shadyak, based on a true story of the doctor's life.

[1] www.uofnkona.edu site, under Mission, Values, History.

CHAPTER 12

[1] Oswald Chambers, *My Utmost for His Highest* (New York: Dodd, Mead, & Co., 1935), Oct. 26 reading.

[2] Janet Hagberg, *Real Power: Stages of Personal Power in Organizations* (Salem, Wis.: Sheffield, 2003), 177–200.

[3] Camille Bishop, "Generational Cohorts and Cultural Diversity as Factors Affecting Leadership Transition in Organizations" (PhD thesis, Trinity Evangelical Divinity School, May 2004).

[4] Ibid.

Howard in 1954 at U of I

This commercial product, which automated the titration process, was introduced in 1955 and was the first public evidence of Howard's passion for automation.

Howard in Kona Harbor, 1983, holding
Eric Franke and looking at YWAM's
new hospital ship, the *Anastasis*

Howard in 1983

Malmstadt family at Camelot in 1992.
From left back row: Jon Malmstadt, Phil Magner, Tom
Bloomer. *Middle row:* Jonathan Magner, Carolyn, Alice
Magner, Cynthia Bloomer, Howard. *Front row:* Paul
Magner, Philippe Bloomer

Howard, Alice, Cynthia, Jon, and Carolyn in 1999

Hands-on electronics kit for the American Chemical
Society Short Course

Stan Crouch, Chris Enke, and
Howard inspecting the short
course electronics kit, 1990